NAGASAKI 1945

NAGASAKI 1945

The first full-length eyewitness account
of the atomic bomb attack on Nagasaki

Tatsuichiro Akizuki

Translated by Keiichi Nagata

Edited and with an introduction by
Gordon Honeycombe

Q

QUARTET BOOKS
LONDON   MELBOURNE   NEW YORK

First published in Great Britain by Quartet Books Limited
1981
A member of the Namara Group
27/29 Goodge Street, London W1P 1FD

ISBN 0 7043 3382 1

British Library Cataloguing in Publication Data
Akizuki, Tatsuichiro
    Nagasaki 1945
    1. Nagasaki – Bombardment, 1945
    I. Title   II. Honeycombe, Gordon
    940.54'26   D767.25.N/
    ISBN 0-7043-3382-1

Filmset, printed and bound in Great Britain by
Hazell Watson & Viney Ltd, Aylesbury, Bucks

Contents

Illustrations

Introduction

by
Gordon Honeycombe

Thirty-six years ago, on 9 August 1945, an atomic bomb, the second ever to be used against humanity, exploded over Nagasaki. Many years later the only full-length eyewitness account of what happened that day and thereafter was written by a Japanese doctor working in a hospital in Nagasaki, Tatsuichiro Akizuki. A paperback edition of his story was published in Japan in 1967 and an English translation, by Keiichi Nagata, which took ten years to make, was privately printed by him in Nagasaki in 1977. Mr Nagata had been a bomber pilot in the war and was a friend of Dr Akizuki; before the war they had both been students at Kyoto University. He dedicated his translation to the men with whom he had served and flown in the war, most of whom had died, to the A-bomb survivors, and to the cause of peace. After the war he became a high-school teacher.

In 1980 I chanced to read Mr Nagata's translation of Dr Akizuki's story. It was a remarkable, moving document, telling me things I had never known or thought about that largely long-forgotten, cataclysmic event a generation ago. It seemed all the more potent and timely when the newspapers were calmly theorizing about the effects of H-bombs, neutron bombs, nuclear weapons of many kinds, and the need for fall-out shelters; when France was boasting of her nuclear strength; when computers in America had twice malfunctioned and put nuclear bombers on full alert; when it was said that South Africa,

Iraq, India, Libya and Israel, in addition to China, Russia, America and Britain, all possessed nuclear weapons with multi-megaton warheads – a thousand times more destructive than an A-bomb. Deaths from nuclear attack were being calculated in millions, areas devastated in hundreds of square miles. It seemed such madness, the more so now that I had read Dr Akizuki's account, now that I was aware of what suffering, pain and death a mere atomic bomb or two had caused, and now that I understood that they need never have been used, nor were they decisive factors in the surrender of Japan. It seemed only right that Dr Akizuki's historic story should be presented to the English-speaking world.

In August 1945, Tatsuichiro Akizuki was twenty-nine, unmarried, and working as a doctor in a small TB hospital which had been established in a Franciscan monastery situated on the northern edge of Nagasaki. Born in the city on 3 January, 1916, he had, after studying medicine at Kyoto University, returned in 1941 to Nagasaki, where he worked in the Radiology Department of Nagasaki Medical College. From there Dr Akizuki went to work in a TB clinic run by Dr Takahara in downtown Nagasaki, and in September 1944, on Dr Takahara's recommendation, he became the resident doctor at Urakami First Hospital. The hospital had been set up in 1942 as an extension of Dr Takahara's clinic and occupied most of the large three-storeyed building that had been founded in 1925 as a Catholic theological school for Japanese priests. It was taken over in 1931 by the Canadian branch of the Order of St Francis. By 1945 very few monks and seminarians or theological students remained in the long and roomy building on Motohara Hill, and it functioned chiefly as a hospital for TB patients.

Before being assigned to the hospital, Dr Akizuki was called up for army service – all doctors under the age of fifty had to enlist. But, having recently been ill with pleurisy and being constitutionally rather weak, he was returned to civilian life after a month of military service. Although one of his six sisters and his younger brother had suffered from TB, he never contracted the disease himself.

Nagasaki was, in August 1945, a large, provincial sea-port

(population 280,000), situated at the head of a long bay on the south-west coast of Japan's southernmost island, Kyushu. Surrounded by mountainous hills, divided in turn by fertile valleys, the city spread up two of the wider valleys from the harbour's complex of shipyards, wharves and port facilities, looking not unlike a smaller, unromantic and unAmericanized version of Hong Kong. The city's main commercial and residential sector, crowded together, sprawled from the sea up the smaller valley; the longer valley was more industrialized, with large steel, engineering and armament factories and workshops dominating the workers' simple homes.

When heavy American bombing of Japan began in 1944, some war industries were dispersed and relocated in schools and in tunnels underground; air-raid shelters were dug out of the hillsides; and the poor, of whom there were many then, became even poorer. Some found a solace in religion, and many of these in the rites, prayers and beliefs of the Catholic Church. For, at that time, Nagasaki had the largest Christian community in Japan. This arose out of the city's long and historic association with the western world; for it was through Nagasaki in the sixteenth century that European merchants and missionaries first entered Japan. But, at the start of the war – Japan attacked Pearl Harbor on 7 December 1941 – that association ended for nearly four years, and resident foreigners, including many Christians of all sects, were immured in concentration camps. An influx of another kind occurred when thousands of Koreans, uprooted from their conquered country, were shipped to Japan and set to work alongside local volunteers, mainly students, high-school pupils and old people, boosting war production. Every fit man was called up to fight. But, by August 1945, the Japanese dream of empire and the establishment of 'The Greater East Asia Co-Prosperity Sphere' was, like Japan itself, in ruins.

Young Dr Akizuki, although often tired by hard work and the privations of wartime Nagasaki, where meat was unobtainable, fish seldom seen and even rice in short supply, was quite ignorant, so thorough were the censors, that Japan was on its knees, defenceless: its navy and air force all but annihilated, its merchant navy all but sunk or disabled, its people near starvation and millions homeless, and over sixty of its cities, like Osaka, Kobe and Nagoya, devastated by American fire-bomb attacks.

Half a million civilians had already been killed, over 100,000 dying on one March night in 1945, when 279 B29 Superfortresses each carrying about seven tons of incendiary bombs, attacked Tokyo. Fifteen square miles of the city were burnt to the ground. In fact, more Japanese civilians were killed by American bombers in one year than died in Germany (593,000) in three years as a result of British and American bombing.

The total of civilian deaths in Britain through bombing was 60,000. In the United States it was less than 100.

Nagasaki was bombed once or twice and strafed; this happened for the first time in April 1945. Being, in effect, the Mitsubishi company town (shipyards, steelworks and armaments), it was a legitimate military target. But although there were air-raid warnings every day, the B29s flew blamelessly over to other targets, like the large air base at Omura twenty miles away (whence suicide planes took off on their fatal missions) and the naval base at Sasebo. Nagasaki was left alone, and its citizens blessed their good fortune, blissfully unaware as they became increasingly careless about air-raid precautions that, as early as May, Nagasaki had already been selected as one of the five cities (the others were Hiroshima, Kokura, Kyoto and Niigata) deemed suitable by the Americans as targets for the atomic bomb. They were suitable because they combined military installations with 'houses and other buildings susceptible to damage'.

President Truman decided as early as June 1945 in favour of dropping the bomb on Japan, if necessary. Few American leaders were consulted, it seems, and few, it seems, approved – although among the Allied leaders Churchill did. Neither Generals Eisenhower, Marshall and MacArthur nor Admirals King and Leahy thought it necessary to use 'this barbaric weapon' – 'that awful thing'. But, as A. J. P. Taylor says: 'Once the bombs were there they had to be used.' Besides, someone had to account for the two billion dollars spent on making them.

No atomic bomb had, however, been tested by the time the war in Europe ended at midnight on 8 May. But, two months later, in New Mexico on 16 July, a plutonium-based atomic bomb was successfully detonated at Alamogordo. Those who were there were stunned at the sight; some rejoiced. 'Now I am become death,' murmured J. Robert Oppenheimer, 'the destroyer of worlds.' Churchill, at the Potsdam Conference, was handed a cryptic message: 'Babies satisfactorily born.' Three days earlier, the Japanese Foreign Office had officially notified the Russians, thought to be neutral mediators, that the Japanese were 'desirous of peace'. Of this the Americans were already well aware, having intercepted and deciphered coded messages between Tokyo and Moscow. But the Western Allies continued to insist on unconditional surrender, which was spiritually and morally unacceptable by Japan, while the two other atomic bombs that had been created – only three were ever made – were transported in pieces to Tinian, an island in the Marianas, south of Saipan, and there assembled.

By then, President Truman and his chief advisors were as bent on using the atomic bomb – avowedly to hasten Japan's surrender and to save bloodshed – as Stalin was on declaring war on Japan to gain as many territorial and political advantages in the Far East as the Russians had already won in Europe. This the other Allies were determined to prevent. There was some temporizing. But an explicit warning to the Japanese and a suggested demonstration of the A-bomb's power – by exploding one over Tokyo Bay – were dismissed. For it was thought that neither idea would have the desired shock-effect produced by the actual devastation of a city. Besides, how embarrassing it would be if the parachute or the intricate mechanisms detonating the bomb failed. Some scientists were also curious to know what effects the bomb would actually have on people.

The Potsdam Declaration of 26 July, outlining the stark terms of unconditional surrender but with no reference to the future status of Emperor Hirohito and threatening 'prompt and utter destruction' unless Japan obeyed, was studied by the Japanese cabinet on 27 July. They decided, while peace negotiations were pursued via Moscow, to 'withhold comment', a phrase that was misinterpreted to the West, where the Allies were told the declaration was not worthy of comment. Truman ordered the A-bomb missions to proceed.

At 8.15 a.m. on Monday, 6 August, a B29 called *Enola Gay*, piloted by USAF Colonel Paul Tibbets, aged twenty-nine – the bombardier was Major Tom Ferebee – dropped a uranium bomb called 'Little Boy' over the city of Hiroshima (population around 300,000). The bomb was accurately dropped over the centre of the city and successfully detonated 560 metres above the ground, the equivalent of 13 kilotons of TNT exploding in the sky.

In the Atlantic, President Truman was speeding back to America on board the cruiser *Augusta*. When he heard the news he exclaimed: 'This is the greatest thing in history!'

NAGASAKI 1945

1

August had been very hot: a series of burning suns. But it was quite cool inside the wards and offices of Urakami Hospital. I had been working at the hospital, which was part of the Franciscan monastery and theological school on Motohara Hill, as the resident doctor since September 1944.

It was easy enough to put up with the heat, but we couldn't escape from the air-raids, repeated day after day, night after night. About eleven o'clock each night I had to tell the patients to take shelter in the basement – it was all part of the daily routine. I was feeling not a little tired.

On the morning of 7 August I unfolded the newspaper as usual. It was a small tabloid that hardly deserved the title of newspaper. I glanced at it, muttering to myself: 'Now, which part of the country was bombed yesterday?'

And then the headline caught my eye: 'New kind of bomb dropped on Hiroshima – Much damage done.' In spite of myself I called to Brother Joseph Iwanaga to take a look – brother Joseph, a Japanese Franciscan monk, aged thirty-six, was at that time in charge of the monastery. Instead of 'incendiary', which regularly appeared in the paper, it said 'new kind of bomb'. Moreover, the paper specified 'much damage done'. This greatly alarmed me. The newspapers and the radio in those days were in the habit of saying 'some slight damage', when referring to the ravages wrought on us both at home and in the various war zones. Now the newspaper openly said 'much damage done', which seemed like a portent of some evil. I stared at the little sheet of paper, holding it very tight.

Wednesday, 8 August was as hot as the day before. In the afternoon, Mr Fujii, a student who was boarding in the monastery's theological school, suddenly hurried back to us from Nagasaki Medical College. 'I've decided to go to Hiroshima,' he said. 'I hear Hiroshima has been completely destroyed. My girlfriend lives in Hiroshima, so I'm going there to see how things are.'

He had good cause to want to visit Hiroshima. That morning he had attended Nagasaki Medical College as usual. At the college all the professors, the staff and the students had been called together for an urgent meeting out of doors, and Dr Tsunoo, the college president, had addressed them. Dr Tsunoo was also president of the National Medical College, a post he had held for twelve years. He often went to Tokyo on official business, and on 7 August happened to pass through Hiroshima on his way back to Nagasaki. Because the railway service had been suspended, he had to make his way across the city centre, and so saw for himself how the whole city had been transformed in an instant into a burnt wasteland. He informed the meeting: 'I'm told there was a great flash, and that at the same time every man and woman was thrown down by a violent blast; houses collapsed and caught fire. The new bomb didn't apparently explode on the ground but in the air. And when it did, a strangely shaped cloud rose into the sky.'

Much agitated, he went on to say how horrifed he had been to see the extent of the destruction wrought on Hiroshima. Standing out on the campus, without any shade from the midsummer sun, he continued: 'This new kind of bomb may also be dropped on Nagasaki, and I feel sure it won't be enough as an air-raid precaution for you to take shelter when you hear enemy planes approaching. Our situation has now become very serious indeed.' You must all, and you students in particular, be more on your guard than ever before and prepare for the worst. As it is, the most terrible devastation has been caused at Hiroshima. There's not a single house or tree left undamaged in an area that encompasses three or four railway stations. It's as if a huge thunderbolt struck the city, or a whirlwind of fire.'

When Mr Fujii told us what President Tsunoo had said, Mr Yoshimi Noguchi, one of the two students who still remained in the monastery's theological school, and I asked in turn:

'I wonder if there *can* be such a terrible bomb?'

'What on earth could have caused such damage?'

I counted the number of stations: one, two, three. That meant that an area about fifteen kilometres square had been burnt to the ground.

In the end, Mr Fujii rejected our advice to stay away and left for Hiroshima, full of anxiety. His fiancée's father was Chief Justice there, and he was impatient to know if she and her family were safe and sound. I said to him before he left: 'It's far too dangerous – you could be killed on the way there.' He set off, with a rucksack on his back. No one knew how fortune smiled on him that afternoon as he left Nagasaki to go to Hiroshima.

The evening of 8 August came, and it was soon dark. Dr Matsunaga, president of the Medical Association in Nagasaki Prefecture, sturdy and strong, and Dr Kuwasaki, president of the Medical Association of Nagasaki City, small and short, both arrived unexpectedly at Urakami Hospital. Something serious must have happened, I thought. However, I was relieved to see them since the hospital was some distance from the city centre, on the hill of Motohara, and I was the only resident doctor responsible for more than seventy tubercular patients.

The day before, Dr Kuwasaki's wife had undergone an operation for acute appendicitis in a city hospital, and because he thought it was dangerous for her to stay in the centre of the town, in case of a fire-bomb attack, he had had his wife removed to our hospital, even though it was still only twenty-four hours or so after her operation. 'She should be safe enough here,' he had said with a smile.

Dr Matsunaga's visit was in connection with another speech by Dr Tsunoo, made at the First-Aid Headquarters in Nagasaki that afternoon. He came all the way to the hospital to tell us about it. The speech, like that reported to us by Mr Fujii, dealt with the destruction of Hiroshima. The obvious power of the new bomb and the tremendous damage it caused greatly dispirited us. That evening, when we had supper, a little later than usual, there was an air of gloom among the staff. Father Paul Ishikawa asked indignantly: 'How long will this useless war and dreadful carnage continue?' And then he was silent, finding solace in meditation and prayer. Brother Iwanaga and I were afraid that the end of humanity would soon steal upon us and upon Japan.

I said: 'Nagasaki and this hospital might be destroyed, but if that happens none of *you* must be injured – we wouldn't have time to treat each other!' I said it jokingly, to break the silence.

Until then, I had no idea of what was meant by an atomic bomb and nuclear energy. Dr Matsunaga knew nothing of these things either. Nor had Dr Tsunoo, the most learned man among us, grasped the meaning of what had happened in Hiroshima, for all he had seen had been its physical destruction. Unknowingly, when he walked through the city, he had, as it turned out, been infected by a large dose of radioactivity. The Japanese people knew little or nothing about the A-bomb. For several years we had been short of commodities and provisions. 'Poverty makes a man dull-witted,' states a proverb, and preoccupied as we were in getting food and seeking shelter in air-raids, we had little or no opportunity for study. All advances in foreign knowledge had been prevented from coming into our country. As I heard later, the American authorities had, however, warned the Japanese government that the A-bomb was a terrible new weapon, that when it exploded something dreadful would happen, and that it would be dropped on Japan before long. But this information was suppressed by some department or other in Japan and never made known. Why were we never informed? – Because certain of our leaders were afraid that, if we knew about the A-bomb, our people would lose their fighting spirit. Japan was rushing blindly towards disaster.

That night I tossed and turned sleeplessly in bed. At eleven, the inevitable air-raid warning sounded over the city. We trooped downstairs, to shelter in the basement. The stars were shining as usual. It was a warm and sultry night.

At midnight on 8 August, Russia declared war on Japan and invaded Manchuria. The order for the second atomic bomb attack on Japan had already been given. At 1.56 a.m., Japanese time, a

B29 Superfortress, No. 77, nicknamed Bock's Car, *took off on its 2,000-mile journey from Tinian to the island of Kyushu, carrying a plutonium bomb more powerful than the one detonated over Hiroshima. The last-minute malfunctioning of a fuel pump, which meant the plane was unable to use its reserve fuel supply, almost caused the cancellation of the trip. But the mission was ordered to proceed.* Bock's Car *was followed by two other B29s which would act as observer planes, one containing cameras and the other instruments for measuring the effects of the explosion. They were to rendezvous over the tiny island of Yakoshima, south of Kyushu.*

The leading B29 took its name from its customary pilot, Fred Bock, and a winged and punning boxcar was painted on its fuselage. On this occasion he happened, however, to be flying the instrument plane, called The Great Artiste. Bock's Car *was piloted by Major Chuck Sweeney, a genial Irish-American from Boston; the second pilot was Captain Don Albury, aged twenty-five. The bombardier, who sat in the Plexiglas nose of the plane, was a young Texan, Captain Kermit Beahan. It was his birthday – he was twenty-seven. There were twelve men on board* Bock's Car: *the ten-man crew and two technical experts. The bomb the plane carried was known as 'Fat Man' because of its cheerful rotundity and consequent association with Churchill. It was 3·5 metres long, weighed 4·5 tons, and had an explosive potential of 22 kilotons of TNT. Their target was Kokura, on the north coast of Kyushu – WP, DV.*

But the weather did not permit nor was God apparently willing that Kokura should enter the history books. As Bock's Car *approached the city at 31,000 feet, its bomb doors open, Kermit Beahan gazed down through the rubber eyepiece of the bomb-sight, waiting for his aiming-point to appear in the cross-sights – the military arsenal. But a heavy industrial haze and smoke from a large fire hid the arsenal from view. He shouted: 'No drop!' The plane banked and approached Kokura again. Beahan saw a river and buildings, but again no arsenal. The plane overshot the target and turned once more. By now it had been observed by citizens far below, a tiny, slow-moving silver fish in the sky. They fled for shelter or paused to look up, wondering at the plane's manoeuvres. Anti-aircraft batteries opened up and flak began to drift up towards the plane. For the third time Sweeney directed* Bock's Car *across the target, and for the third time Kermit Beahan failed* to see the aiming-point beneath its protecting mantle of smoky haze. Following official instructions to the letter, he again shouted: 'No drop!' Sweeney had a problem: fighters as well as flak were climbing up towards the plane's great height, and fuel was running low. He abandoned Bock's Car's primary objective and turned towards the secondary alternative – Nagasaki.

The deteriorating fuel situation meant that the plane was now unable to return to Tinian and might not make it back to Okinawa. Sweeney realized there was not even enough fuel for more than one run over the other city. Then he learned that a front of thin cloud was moving in over Nagasaki from the East China Sea.

The plane flew south, turning to approach the city from the sea, flying at 29,000 feet up the harbour approaches. Again the area was obscured, this time by puffy white clouds. The plane approached and passed the cloud-hidden target at the head of the harbour, and as it did so a rift appeared in the clouds beneath, revealing the oval outline of a stadium. Kermit Beahan made some instantaneous adjustments and aligned the cross-bars of his bomb-sight on the stadium below. He pressed the button.

'Bombs away!' he said. 'Bomb away.'

Bock's Car groaned as, released of its burden, it veered to the left, roaring high above Urakami Hospital and heading for an eventual emergency landing on Okinawa.

'Fat Man' fell silently and slowly under its parachute, one and a half miles adrift of its target. It fell for forty seconds. And in the forty seconds every move that people chose to make below became of vital importance, a choice between life and death, between degrees of pain and grief. Five hundred metres above the city the bomb detonated. It was 11.02 a.m.

On Thursday, 9 August, the boundless blue sky, the loud shrilling of cicadas, promised another day as hot and as sultry as the day before.

At 8.30 I began the medical examination and treatment of out-patients. Nearly thirty had turned up by ten o'clock. Some were patients requiring artificial pneumo-thorax (the temporary collapsing of a lung); they had been entrusted to us by Takahara Hospital, 5,000 metres away. Miss Yoshioka, a woman doctor in her mid-thirties who came from there, arrived to assist me with the operations, as well as two nurses also belonging to Takahara Hospital. Our hospital was in something of a turmoil.

During the morning Mr Yokota turned up to see his daughter, who was one of our in-patients. He lived at the foot of Motohara Hill, and was an engineer in the research department of the Mitsubishi Ordnance Factory, then one of the centres of armament manufacture in Japan. The torpedoes used in the attack on Pearl Harbor had been made there. Mr Yokota always had something interesting to say. He used to visit me now and again, often passing on some new piece of scientific information.

He said: 'I hear Hiroshima was very badly damaged on the sixth.'

Together we despaired over the destiny of Japan, he as an engineer, I as a doctor.

Then he said gloomily: 'I don't think the explosion was caused by any form of chemical energy.'

'What then?' I inquired, eager to know about the cause of the explosion, even though my patients were waiting for me.

He said: 'The power of the bomb dropped on Hiroshima is far stronger than any accumulation of chemical energy produced by the dissolution of a nitrogren compound, such as nitro-glycerine. It was an *atomic* bomb, produced by atomic fission.'

'Good heavens! At last we have atomic fission!' I said, though somewhat doubtfully.

Just then the long continuous wail of a siren arose.

'Listen . . . Here comes the regular air-raid.'

'The first warning . . . The enemy are on their way.'

Mr Yokota hurried back down the hill to his factory and all at once I began to feel nervous. It was now about 10.30. When such a warning sounded we were supposed to make sure our patients took refuge in our basement air-raid shelter. We were meant to do likewise. But recently I had become so accustomed to air-raids that, even though it was somewhat foolhardy, I no longer bothered with every precaution. In any case, breakfast was about to begin. At the time our diet at the hospital consisted of two meals a day of unpolished rice. The patients were waiting for their breakfast to be served, and so remained on the second and third floors.

I went out of the building. It was very hot. The sky had clouded over a little but the familiar formation of B29 bombers was neither to be seen nor heard. I asked myself: 'What route will our dear enemies choose to take today?'

I went in again to warn my patients to stay away from the windows – they could be swept by machine-gun fire. Recently we had been shot up once or twice by fighter-planes from American aircraft carriers in neighbouring waters.

About thirty minutes later the all-clear sounded. I said to myself: In Nagasaki everything is still all right. *Im Westen Nichts Neues* – All quiet on the Western Front.

I went down to the consulting room, humming cheerfully. Now that the all-clear had been given I felt free from danger. I entered the room and found Dr Yoshioka about to carry out an artificial pneumo-thorax operation on one of the male out-patients. 'You ought to stop working when the air-raid warning goes, at least for a little while,' I told her.

'Thank you,' she replied. 'But there were so many patients waiting.'

She looked tired. She had come to the hospital that morning on foot, walking 5,000 metres across Nagasaki, and since then she had been very busy treating the patients who needed attention.

'Please have a rest,' I said. 'I'll carry on in your place.'

'Well . . . Thank you for your kindness,' she said, and went upstairs to her room to rest. I began the pneumo-thorax. Miss Sugako Murai, one of our few trained nurses, was there by my side to help me. She was two years younger than me and came from Koshima in Nagasaki; she had been at Urakami Hospital for about four months, since April.

It was eleven o'clock. Father Ishikawa, who was Korean, aged about thirty-six and the hospital chaplain, was listening in the hospital chapel to the confessions of those Catholics who had gone to him to confess, one after the other, before the great festival, on 15 August, of the Ascension of the Virgin Mary, which was only a week away. Brother Joseph Iwanaga was toiling outside the hospital with some farm workers, digging another air-raid shelter in the shrubbery in the centre of the hospital yard. Mr Noguchi had just begun to repair the apparatus used to lift water from the well. Other members of staff were busy providing a late breakfast. Some were filling big bowls with miso soup; others were carrying them through the corridors or up the stairs. The hospital was a hive of activity after the all-clear.

'Well, we'll soon be getting our breakfast,' I said to Miss Murai. 'The patients must be hungry.'

So was I, but before we had our breakfast we would have to finish treating all the out-patients.

I stuck the pneumo-thorax needle into the side of the chest of the patient lying on the bed. It was just after 11 a.m.

I heard a low droning sound, like that of distant aeroplane engines.

'What's that?' I said. 'The all-clear has gone, hasn't it?'

At the same time the sound of the plane's engines, growing louder and louder, seemed to swoop down over the hospital.

I shouted: 'It's an enemy plane! Look out – take cover!'

As I said so, I pulled the needle out of the patient and threw myself beside the bed.

There was a blinding white flash of light, and the next moment – *Bang! Crack!* A huge impact like a gigantic blow smote down upon our bodies, our heads and our hospital. I lay flat – I didn't know whether or not of my own volition. Then down came piles of debris, slamming into my back.

The hospital has been hit, I thought. I grew dizzy, and my ears sang.

Some minutes or so must have passed before I staggered to my feet and looked around. The air was heavy with yellow smoke; white flakes of powder drifted about; it was strangely dark.

Thank God, I thought – I'm not hurt! But what about the patients?

As it became brighter, little by little our situation grew clearer. Miss Murai, who had been assisting me with the pneumo-thorax, struggled to her feet beside me. She didn't seem to have been seriously injured, though she was completely covered with white dust. 'Hey, cheer up!' I said. 'We're not hurt, thank God!'

I helped her to her feet. Another nurse, who was also in the consulting room, and the patient, managed to stand up. The man, his face smeared white like a clown and streaked with blood, lurched towards the door, holding his bloody head with his hands and moaning.

I said to myself over and over again: Our hospital has suffered a direct hit – We've been bombed! Because the hospital stood on a hill and had walls of red brick, it must, I thought, have attracted the attention of enemy planes. I felt deeply and personally responsible for what had happened.

The pervading dingy yellow silence of the room now resounded with faint cries – 'Help!' The surface of the walls and ceiling had peeled away. What I had thought to be clouds of dust or smoke was whirling brick-dust and plaster. Neither the pneumo-thorax apparatus nor the microscope on my desk were anywhere to be seen. I felt as if I were dreaming.

I encouraged Miss Murai, saying: 'Come on, we haven't been hurt at all, by the grace of God. We must rescue the in-patients.' But privately I thought it must be all over with them – the second and third floors must have disintegrated, I thought.

We went to the door of the consulting room which faced the main stairway, and there were the in-patients coming down the steps, crying: 'Help me, doctor! Oh, help me, sir.' The stairs and the corridor were heaped with timbers, plaster, debris from the ceiling. It made walking difficult. The patients staggered down towards us, crying: 'I'm hurt! Help me!' Strangely, none seemed to have been seriously injured, only slightly wounded, with fresh blood dripping from their faces and hands.

If the bomb had actually hit the hospital, I thought, they would have been far more badly injured.

'What's happened to the second and third floors?' I cried. But all they answered was – 'Help me! Help!'

One of them said: 'Mr Yamaguchi has been buried under the debris. Help him.'

No one knew what had happened. A huge force had been released above our heads. What it was, nobody knew. Had it been several tons of bombs, or the suicidal destruction of a plane carrying a heavy bomb-load?

Dazed, I retreated into the consulting room, in which the only upright object on the rubbish-strewn floor was my desk. I went and sat on it and looked out of the window at the yard and the outside world. There was not a single pane of glass in the window, not even a frame – all had been completely blown away. Out in the yard dun-coloured smoke or dust cleared little by little. I saw figures running. Then, looking to the south-west, I was stunned. The sky was as dark as pitch, covered with dense clouds of smoke; under that blackness, over the earth, hung a yellow-brown fog. Gradually the veiled ground became visible, and the view beyond rooted me to the spot with horror.

All the buildings I could see were on fire: large ones and small ones and those with straw-thatched roofs. Further off along the valley, Urakami Church, the largest Catholic church in the east, was ablaze. The technical school, a large two-storeyed wooden building, was on fire, as were many houses and the distant ordnance factory. Electricity poles were wrapped in flame like so many pieces of kindling. Trees on the near-by hills were smoking, as were the leaves of sweet potatoes in the fields. To say that everything burned is not enough. It seemed as if the earth itself emitted fire and smoke, flames that writhed up and erupted from underground. The sky was dark, the ground was scarlet, and in between hung clouds of yellowish smoke. Three kinds of colour – black, yellow and scarlet – loomed ominously over the people, who ran about like so many ants seeking to escape. What had happened? Urakami Hospital had not been bombed — I understood that much. But that ocean of fire, that sky of smoke! It seemed like the end of the world.

I ran out into the garden. Patients who were only slightly hurt came up to me, pleading for aid.

I shouted at them: 'For heaven's sake! You're not seriously wounded!'

One patient said: 'Kawaguchi and Matsuo are trapped in their rooms! They can't move. You must help them!'

I said to myself: Yes, we must first of all rescue those seriously ill tubercular patients who've been buried under the ruins.

I looked southwards again, and the sight of Nagasaki city in a sea of flames as far as the eye could reach made me think that such destruction could only have been caused by thousands of bombers, carpet-bombing. But not a plane was to be seen or heard, although even the leaves of potatoes and carrots at my feet were scorched and smouldering. The electricity cables must have exploded underground, I thought.

And then at last I identified the destroyer – 'That's it!' I cried. 'It was the new bomb – the one used on Hiroshima!'

'Look – there's smoke coming from the third floor!' exclaimed one of the patients, who had fled for safety into the hospital yard.

I turned about and looked up at the roof.

The hospital was built of brick and reinforced concrete, but the main roof was tiled, sloping in the Japanese style, and in the middle of the roof was another small, ridged roof, from whose end a little smoke was issuing, as if something was cooking there. Almost all the tiles had fallen off, leaving the roof timbers exposed.

That's odd, I said to myself, not heeding what I saw.

The smoke from the hospital looked just like that of a cigarette in comparison with the masses billowing above the technical school, Urakami Church, near-by houses, and the Convent of the Holy Cross, which were now blazing with great ferocity. The sky was dark, as if it were threatening to rain.

'As soon as we have some rain,' I said, 'these fires will quickly be extinguished.' So saying, I began to dash about in the confusion.

The fire in the hospital roof spread little by little. It was rather strange how the roof was the first thing in the hospital to catch fire. But the temperature at the instant the bomb exploded would have been thousands of degrees Centigrade at the epicentre and hundreds of degrees Centigrade near the hospital. Wooden buildings within 1,500 metres of the epicentre instantly caught fire. Within 1,000 metres, iron itself melted. The hospital stood 1,800 metres away from the epicentre. Probably, coming on top of the scorching heat of the sun, which had shone for more than ten days running, the blasting breath of hundreds of degrees Centigrade had dried out the hospital timbers and ignited them. The attics under the roof were wooden and used as a store-house; the fire now spread through them. Upset as I was, at first I wasn't too concerned, thinking it was only a small fire. But before long the main roof of the building was enveloped in flames.

'Doctor! Doctor!' people shouted. 'There are still many patients on the third floor!'

I went up to the third floor many times, and ran down just as often. As I rushed about like a madman, the damage sustained by the hospital became much clearer. Brother Iwanaga and Mr Noguchi, who were both fit and well, also raced up and down in the work of rescue.

'Dr Yoshioka has been badly hurt. I'm afraid she's going to die.'

That cry was heard several times, and it so discouraged me that, for a while, my feet would hardly move.

I also heard someone say: 'Brother Iwanaga is taking Dr Yoshioka to the hill opposite the hospital, carrying her on his back. Please come quickly, sir!'

Another voice cried from somewhere a bit later: 'The chief nurse has been injured, and is being taken to the hill where Dr Yoshioka is.'

Meanwhile we were carrying those patients who were seriously ill down from the third floor, even as the fire was spreading along the hospital roof. But thanks to the unselfish devotion of the nurses and the co-operation of the in-patients, we were able to bring out all the serious tubercular cases, until only two remained. Pinned under fallen beams, they could not be pulled away, despite all our efforts. At that point I came close to running away myself, to giving them up in despair. But something had to be tried to rescue them. Brother Iwanaga and Mr Noguchi brought a saw with which we cut through the beams until at last the two could be freed.

Miss Murai wept with happiness, overjoyed that no patients would now be burnt to death in the hospital.

'We have rescued every one of them!' she cried.

Ten or twenty minutes after the smoke had cleared outside, people began coming up the hill from the town below, crying out and groaning: 'Help me, help!' Those cries and groans seemed not to be made by human voices; they sounded unearthly, weird.

About ten minutes after the explosion, a big man, half-naked, holding his head between his hands, came into the yard towards me, making sounds that seemed to be dragged from the pit of his stomach.

'Got hurt, sir,' he groaned; he shivered as if he were cold. 'I'm hurt.'

I stared at him, at the strange-looking man. Then I saw it was Mr Zenjiro Tsujimoto, a market-gardener and a friendly neighbour to me and the hospital. I wondered what had happened to the robust Zenjiro.

'What's the matter with you, Tsujimoto?' I asked him, holding him in my arms.

'In the pumpkin field over there – getting pumpkins for the

patients – got hurt . . .' he said, speaking brokenly and breathing feebly.

It was all he could do to keep standing. Yet it didn't occur to me that he had been seriously injured.

'Come along now,' I said. 'You are perfectly all right, I assure you. Where's your shirt? Lie down and rest somewhere where it's cool. I'll be with you in a moment.'

His head and his face were whitish; his hair was singed. It was because his eyelashes had been scorched away that he seemed so bleary-eyed. He was half-naked because his shirt had been burned from his back in a single flash. But I wasn't aware of such facts. I gazed at him as he reeled about with his head between his hands. What a change had come over this man who was stronger than a horse, whom I had last seen earlier that morning. It's as if he's been struck by lightning, I thought.

After Mr Tsujimoto came staggering up to me, another person who looked just like him wandered into the yard. Who he was and where he had come from I had no idea. 'Help me,' he said, groaning, half-naked, holding his head between his hands. He sat down, exhausted. 'Water . . . Water . . .' he whispered.

'What's the trouble? What's wrong with you? What's become of your shirt?' I demanded.

'Hot – *hot* . . . Water . . . I'm burning.' They were the only words that were articulate.

As time passed, more and more people in a similar plight came up to the hospital – ten minutes, twenty minutes, an hour after the explosion. All were of the same appearance, sounded the same. 'I'm hurt, *hurt*! I'm burning! Water!' They all moaned the same lament. I shuddered. Half-naked or stark naked, they walked with strange, slow steps, groaning from deep inside themselves as if they had travelled from the depths of hell. They looked whitish; their faces were like masks. I felt as if I were dreaming, watching pallid ghosts processing slowly in one direction – as in a dream I had once dreamt in my childhood.

These ghosts came on foot uphill towards the hospital, from the direction of the burning city and from the more easterly ordnance factory. Worker or student, girl or man, they all walked slowly and had the same mask-like face. Each one groaned and cried for help. Their cries grew in strength as the people increased in number, sounding like something from the Buddhist scriptures, re-echoing everywhere, as if the earth itself were in pain.

One victim who managed to reach the hospital yard asked me, 'Is this a hospital?' before suddenly collapsing on the ground. There were those who lay stiffly where they fell by the roadside in front of the hospital; others lay in the sweet-potato fields. Many went down to the steep valley below the hospital where a stream ran down between the hill of Motohara and the next hill. 'Water, water,' they cried. They went instinctively down to the banks of the stream, because their bodies had been scorched and their throats were parched and inflamed; they were thirsty. I didn't realize then that these were the symptoms of 'flashburn'.

Many times I met with and separated from Brother Iwanaga as each of us toiled wherever we happened to be. Earlier, Brother Iwanaga had rescued a farmer, Mr Yamano, by sawing through the boughs of a tree that had fallen upon him in the yard. Now Brother Iwanaga said to me: 'Father Ishikawa has been hurt, some part of his head.'

After mass that morning Father Ishikawa had listened to the confessions of the Catholics, who had grown in number as the festival of the Ascension of the Virgin Mary approached. Towards eleven o'clock, he had returned to his room on the third floor to fetch a book he needed, and then hurried back to the chapel. He was passing along the corridor in the middle of the first floor when a sudden white flash filled the corridor with light; there was a great roar and he was hurled head over heels through the air, striking his head against a concrete post. But although he was in some pain, he returned to the chapel, where such thick yellowish smoke and white dust hung over the broken furnishings he could hardly tell where he was. Not a person was in sight. It was there that Brother Iwanaga found him. When I saw Father Ishikawa, lying down in a shaded part of the yard, one of his eyes had swollen purple. Fortunately, the bleeding from his injured head had stopped.

Black smoke was now billowing up from the hospital roof. By the time the rescue of all the patients had been achieved, the top floor was enveloped in smoke and the fire in the roof burned furiously.

'Ah, the X-ray machines will be burnt!' I exclaimed, in spite of myself.

Miss Murai and some of the patients took up my cry. We had thought the fire would be held back by the ceiling of the third floor, which was made of thick concrete. But when a lift was installed in the hospital, a shaft three metres square had been built in the middle of the building, from the basement to the third floor. Into that shaft burning timbers now fell, crashing down into the basement, where three of the most up-to-date X-ray machines were stored, Half of the best X-ray machines in Nagasaki city were, in fact, in the care of our hospital, thought to be the safest place for them. In the transformer of every X-ray machine there was a quantity of insulation oil. The transformers blew up in the intense heat and the machines caught fire.

'There they go,' I murmured sadly.

The sun shone dim and reddish through the south-westerly veil of black smoke over the city. It seemed a long time since the explosion. I thought it must now be evening, but only three hours had passed. It was just two o'clock and still broad daylight. I had completely lost any sense of time. And I was not alone – it was a timeless day for everyone. It seemed as if years had passed, maybe because so many houses continued to burn and because so many badly injured people appeared one after another before my eyes. On the other hand, it felt as if only a moment had passed, because all around us people and houses and fields seemed unbelievably changed.

Not every part of the hospital was beset with fire. Brother Iwanaga and I went in and out of the building many times, for I still had to make sure that all the patients and staff were safe and to check for any dead or wounded. We couldn't imagine how everything had looked before the explosion – rooms, corridors, furniture and the rest. The ceilings had all been stripped of their planks and plaster, the walls of their panelling. Desks, cupboards, bookcases, instrument boxes, medicine chests had all been overturned. Whatever had escaped the onslaught had been emptied – drawers were open and their contents lost. I never found out what happened to the contents of my desk. A gigantic wind had struck the hospital, shattered the windows, torn through every room, swept along the corridors and ravaged everything inside the hospital with a force beyond human comprehension.

It is the mark of the devil, I thought – of the devil's claw.

Clothes which the chief nurse and the nurses once wore were lying about as if torn off their bodies. The mere sight of them made me afraid that they had been killed. But in fact it was only that the door of the wardrobe in the room had been torn off and the clothing inside blown out.

I noticed other unusual facts. The ceremonial robes usually kept by the altar in the chapel were discovered far away, torn to shreds. The books from the library were scattered in unimaginable places. As for my own office, where many important records and instruments were kept – the whole room had been wrecked. I couldn't find a thing. The clothes I had put on that morning were all that remained of my possessions. My shoes were straw sandals. I felt uneasy about them. There had been three pairs of fine leather shoes in my room, but I couldn't find any of them, hard as I tried. In the end I ran about for several days with only straw sandals on my feet. My soles must have been infected by radioactivity but I was unaware of the danger.

In the afternoon a change was noticeable in the appearance of the injured people who came up to the hospital. The crowd of ghosts which had looked whitish in the morning were now burned black. Their hair was burnt; their skin, which was charred and blackened, blistered and peeled. Such were those who now came toiling up to the hospital yard and fell there weakly.

'Are you a doctor? Please, if you wouldn't mind, could you examine me?' So said a young man.

'Cheer up!' I said. It was all I could say.

He died in the night. He must have been one of the many medical students who were injured down at the medical college. His politeness and then his poor blackened body lying dead on the concrete are things I shall never forget.

Neither shall I ever forget the countenance of a father who came stumbling up to me, carrying his baby in his arms. The father begged me to try to do something for his baby. I examined the child. The wall of its stomach had been sliced open and part of its intestines protruded. The baby's face was purple. No pulse could be felt.

I said, 'It's hopeless.'

The father, laying his baby on the grass in the yard, sat down exhausted and said: 'Would you do what you can?'

I shook my head. There was nothing that I could do. I had neither medical instruments nor medicine. He wouldn't leave the child.

The brick wall around the hospital was in ruins, blown down by the blast. The wall, hundreds of metres long, had like everything else been crushed by a devilish force. A child who had been playing near the wall lay beneath it on the road, his skull broken like a pomegranate.

Gradually the severity of cases increased: a person whose body had been riven by pieces of glass or splinters blown by the colossal force of the blast; a person who had been battered by heavy objects falling upon him; a person who had been blown off his feet and thrown against something hard – people with such serious injuries appeared one after the other. None of them, however, knew how they had come to be so badly injured. They all trembled with fear and pain, each thinking that the bomb had fallen only on them.

The southern sky was still dark. After the strange clouds caused by the explosion had thinned, smoke from the burning city obscured the sky. Through it the sun shone redly now and again. Sometimes the sound of aeroplane engines could be heard overhead – not Japanese planes, but those of the enemy. Because of the smoke, we couldn't see them. The droning sound of the enemy's low-altitude flights was repeated several times, and every time the sound was heard the injured trembled, fled and hid, fearing that another bomb would be dropped or that machine-gun fire would sweep through them. Whenever the sound of the engines was heard we stopped whatever we were doing and hid, thinking the enemy were about to attack again with even greater ferocity.

I thought it unlikely, however, that they would drop any more bombs on us after the new bomb. Possibly the planes were flying over on reconnaissance, checking on the damage the bomb had done. But the injured who ran about below, seeking to survive any further attack, and the people caring for the injured could not reason as objectively as I. The throb of engines made all of us tremble and cower, and the hateful sound continued off and on, endlessly, as it would do even through the night, droning above the city where the black smoke hung in heavy clouds.

'Isn't all this destruction enough?' I cried, and bit my lip in mortification.

'Miss Yoshioka is about to die from loss of blood.'

I heard this repeated again and again as the day went on. One consolation in our misery was that Brother Iwanaga, Miss Murai and the two young seminarians, Mr Noguchi and Mr Matsuda weren't injured, though all were much shaken by the disaster. Now and then we would meet up with one another, but soon parted again. Miss Murai, however, remained at my side.

'I'm afraid Dr Yoshioka will die,' said Mr Noguchi, on one of his periodic reports back to me. Now that all the in-patients had been carried out and there was nobody left in the hospital, I had time to be more concerned about her.

'None of *you* must be injured – we wouldn't have time to treat each other.' I was reminded of the words I had spoken in jest only yesterday. It now seemed as if I would shortly be in attendance on Dr Yoshioka's death. An image of her overlapped with that of the baby with the lacerated stomach, with that of the charred, empurpled medical student whom I had seen not long ago.

In front of the hospital there was a rice field, beyond which flowed the stream, about two metres wide, by the hill of Motohara. To the east of the stream stood a steep hill covered with trees, which belonged to Mr Mizoguchi. The trees grew thickly and from among them gushed a cold clear spring, running down to the stream below. The people who lived in Motohara called the spring water, 'Water-to-moisten-a-dying-man's-lips'.

Unsteadily, desperately trying to pull myself together, I went down to the stream with Mr Noguchi.

'Where's Dr Yoshioka?' I asked him.

'She's lying in the woods on the hill, attended by the chief nurse, Miss Fukahori,' he replied.

When I reached the little river, I came across an astonishing scene. Half-naked or nearly naked people were crouching at the water's edge. All looked alike, without distinction of sex or age; long hair was the only clue to the female sex. On one side their bodies had been grilled and were highly inflamed. The procession of white ghosts which had passed me some time before had gathered here on the bank of the stream, seeking water to relieve the terrible thirst and the scorching pain of their bodies. Crowds of these victims lined the stream.

'Oh, how it hurts! I'm hurting – burning!' said Mr Tsujimoto, groaning. His face, which had been whitish, when I saw him earlier, was now darker, blackened; his lips were swollen. His wife sat not far away, her face and body also blackened, moaning insensibly.

'Don't drink any water!' I cried.

Everyone turned their faces towards me. Many of them I knew, including several women who belonged to the Convent of the Holy Cross. They had been weeding in the rice fields, trimming the tendrils in the fields of sweet potatoes. When the all-clear sounded, they returned to their labours, just before the explosion. The moment they turned to look up at the sound of the plane, their faces as well as their backs were burnt by the flash, the temperature of the explosion being several hundred degrees Centigrade even in our neighbourhood.

It seemed to me like a picture of hell, seeing those groaning, half-naked people, cinder-burnt, sitting here and there about the stream where the rushes grew. They all called out: 'Doctor! Doctor!' Promising to bring some medicaments to them later, I hurried on up to the trees, where several kinds of oak grew and the air was cooler. I came up to Dr Yoshioka. 'Are you in pain?' I asked.

She and the chief nurse, Miss Tsuyako Fukahori, aged forty-two, looked up at me as if reproaching me for being so long in coming. A cloth had been wound round and round Dr Yoshioka's head, so that only one of her eyes was peering out.

I said: 'You're bandaged very nicely. I see the bleeding has stopped.'

Miss Fukahori and Mr Noguchi had stopped the bleeding. Dr Yoshioka's pulse was firm enough. She was not too pale.

'She's not in any danger,' I said. 'I'm afraid there's nothing else I can do for her.'

Miss Fukahori pointed at the hospital and said: 'It's burning! The hospital's on fire.' It lay across the narrow valley on a level with us. The flames were still gaining strength, and smoke poured out of the upper windows. A strong three-storeyed concrete building won't burn down so easily, I said to myself, even if everything inside it burns. But at least every patient's life has been saved.

A little way off I noticed a man lying among the trees. His face had also been charred. It was Mr Kinoshita. His wife knelt beside him, looking after him, a baby on her back. He was panting heavily. Mr Kinoshita was a teacher at Yamazato Primary School. At the moment of the explosion most of the teachers, together with students from the senior class, were digging an air-raid shelter in the playground and carrying the soil away, their bodies all in a sweat. In an instant they were burnt and blown down by the bomb's colossal blast and heat. The teachers and the students, calling the names of their friends and fellows, ran off in all directions. Anxious about his family, Mr Kinoshita managed to find his way to the house near Motohara hill where he and his family lived. When he got there he found the house in ruins and his family nowhere to be seen. His wife then happened to find him, and they both sought refuge among the trees up on the hill. He was breathing with some difficulty, and gasping for water in his thirst. His wife, kneeling beside him, was quite distraught.

Wretchedly she asked: 'Doctor, what shall I do?'

Pointing to the burning hospital, I said: 'When the fire is over I'll go and find some medicines. Please wait till then.'

It was all I could do – make empty promises. I advised her to bathe his body with any kind of oil.

She said: 'Can he eat these, sir?' She had several cucumbers with her which had come from the farm.

I said: 'Yes, he can.'

He ate them in poor spirits. I ate one too. I had eaten nothing since morning. Mr Kinoshita's face seemed to turn purple little by little. I'll come back to him soon, I said to myself. Then I returned to Dr Yoshioka.

'Keep your spirits up,' I said and set out for the hospital, passing Dr Kuwasaki's wife sitting by the stream. She hadn't been injured, but was now much distressed. It was only three days since she had her appendectomy.

I came across young Mr Kawano, a medical student, in the hospital yard. He was wearing a shirt and some shorts and had a towel around his head. He had been slightly injured in the head; from the wound some blood still seeped. In his arms he was carrying a baby boy.

'What's the matter with the child? Has he been hurt? How about the college, and the college hospital?' I rattled off these questions one after the other.

'The college has been completely destroyed,' he answered simply. 'The city is a sea of flames. All the way up here I saw heaps of dead bodies.' His voice was quite calm.

He told me that, at the medical college, Professor Koyano came into the consulting room just before eleven o'clock to give a lecture to the fourth-year students. Mr Kawano said that before that the professor had been chatting with a group of medical students in an ante-room. Professor Koyano then began his examination of a patient; the students surrounded him; Mr Kawano stood directly behind him. The professor was carefully explaining some medical point when a vivid white flash and a violent blast struck the medical college. Both Professor Koyano and Mr Kawano were thrown down. Some time later, Mr Kawano got away from the building, pursued by the smoke, the heat and the cries of people.

The medical college was built of wood. It had been constructed in the Taisho era, in the 1920s. The hospital itself was a strong concrete building, built in the Showa era, in the 1930s. Mr Kawano only just managed to escape from the smoke of the burning college. The pleasant wooden building, with its illustrious reputation, had collapsed like a trodden frog, from whose back the flames were rising. Even the interior of the concrete hospital was by then blazing like a furnace.

As Mr Kawano ran away from the inferno he came across an infant boy crying beside a wrecked house. He went up to the boy and took him by the hand. As he did so a woman's voice came from under the fallen roof-tiles and timbers: 'Please help – help my child! Save him, save him!'

'I could hear her voice,' said Mr Kawano, 'but I couldn't see her. I only saw part of her legs. The rest of her body was buried under the beams, bricks and tiles. There was no one near-by to help me dig her out of the wreckage. Flames were breaking out a few metres away.' Mr Kawano hardened himself against feelings of pity and shouted: 'Don't worry! He'll be all right! I'll take care of your child!'

Leaving the mother to her fate, he ran as best he could towards the higher ground with other refugees. Among the crackling, crunching, roaring of the fire, among the shrieks of those who were trapped, the screams of those who were being burnt alive, in the midst of those agonizing cries the mother's words of thanks had been hardly audible: 'Thank you . . . Please . . . take care of him . . .'

Feeling entirely responsible for the child, he had set out for Urakami Hospital on the hill of Motohara. He said to himself: I hope that the staff there and the in-patients haven't been injured; the hospital is far from the fire, and besides, it stands on a hill and has an open yard; I'll leave the child in their care.

After he passed the shattered flaming pile of Urakami Church he crossed a stream called the river Motoo. The scene there was like some vision of hell. In the stream itself people lay heaped on top of each other; a mother and child were locked in each other's arms, both naked; a mother and her foetus, still connected by its umbilical cord, were both dead. The pregnant woman must have been burnt and tried to flee; when she jumped into the river she must have given birth.

When at last Mr Kawano reached the hill of Motohara, he came across the procession of white, burnt ghosts. It was about three o'clock when he reached the hospital, carrying the child.

I said to him: 'Why on earth did you bring this child here, when there are countless people to be taken care of? The in-patients, the staff – there are many injured and dead around here.' I spoke savagely. 'Why have you brought the child here? Who will take care of it? He needs milk!'

No matter what I said he continued to nurse the child. Meanwhile, the little boy, whose head was bloody, kept on crying. Eventually Mr Kawano set the child down on the grass. Some of the women in-patients took care of him, although his crying still echoed about the yard.

Mr Kawano then began to feel better, and he soon became one of the most valuable men at Urakami Hospital; he was twenty-seven. He devoted himself to the care of the patients, carrying them from place to place, and he assisted Brother Iwanaga and others in fire-fighting. He had studied Protestant theology before joining the army. He then entered Nagasaki Medical College so that he might master the science of medicine. His view of life, influenced by his Protestant beliefs, was to prove to be most useful to us all.

'What's become of your mother?' Miss Murai asked as I hurried to and fro among the injured.

'She's probably been burnt,' I answered over my shoulder, dismissively, and dashed towards whatever voice was calling me.

When I visited Dr Yoshioka, she and Miss Fukahori had also inquired: 'Have you found out anything about your mother?' 'No,' I said. 'She's probably been burnt. I don't know what's happened to her.' I answered them curtly, with apparent indifference.

To tell the truth, I was very apprehensive about my mother's fate. My parents were still vigorous, despite their age; but during the war, as life in the centre of Nagasaki became more dangerous, they moved much nearer to Urakami Hospital. For two months now they had been living in a farmer's house which stood within a stone's throw of the hospital. They looked after themselves, and each morning my father went to work as a scrivener in the law-courts, writing and formulating legal letters, pleas and bills, as he had done for forty years, and every morning my mother was left alone in the house. I was seldom able to visit them, as I was much occupied with the care of my patients day and night.

In the hours that passed after the bomb was dropped, I became increasingly anxious about my mother. When I looked northwest through the hospital's empty windows, the farmer's house where my mother lived was hidden by fire and smoke. Those who had been working in the rice fields below the hospital had been burnt black. Those who had been in their houses had been crushed beneath them and swallowed up by flames. Taking everything into consideration, I thought she must either have been crushed out of hand, or else burnt to cinders. Every time I saw an old woman who had been burnt among the crowds of people at the hospital, I thought it was Mother.

Miss Murai frequently suggested: 'Let's go and look for your mother.'

Each time I shook my head and said: 'If she's dead, I'd rather know about it as late as possible.'

In my mind I had given my mother up for lost. I continued to hurry hither and thither in response to the cries of the injured, as if possessed by some demon. Then, as I tumbled out of the burning hospital and into the yard for the umpteenth time, I bumped into Miss Murai. She was leading my mother forward by the hand.

Seeing Mother smile at me, I couldn't speak a word. Her smiling face seemed like an image in a dream.

'Your mother hasn't been hurt at all!' said Miss Murai. 'She was in an air-raid shelter.'

'You've not been hurt either!' That was all that Mother said.

I said nothing. I couldn't believe in her miraculous deliverance. My eyes filled with tears; my mother's smile faltered. Miss Murai began to weep. It was shortly after three o'clock in the afternoon of that day.

Later, I learned what had happened. After my father had gone to work, my mother watched the people who were working in the fields belonging to the hospital and weeded the forecourt of her home. When the air-raid siren sounded, she entered the air-raid shelter with the others. When the all-clear went, the farm-workers returned to their labours outside. As her eyesight was somewhat poor, she sat down at the entrance to the shelter, alert for any further danger, even after the all-clear. At 11.02 she heard the unexpected sound of a plane and was so alarmed she hastened inside the shelter. At that moment a great shock-wave and blinding flash of light struck the fields. She had already entered the shelter, so was not directly exposed to either; but she felt their great power and sensed the great changes they effected above her head. When smoke drifted down into the shelter she became frightened and scurried out, only to be deeply shocked at the fearful alteration to the once familiar scene. When she saw all the buildings about her on fire and thick black smoke rising from the distant hospital, she feared that her son must have died.

Now mother and son were reunited, and neither were injured. We did nothing but smile at each other in silence, saying nothing and silently rejoicing in each other's arms. Each had believed the other to be certainly dead. Now, as we met together on the burnt ground, I came to a decision. From this point on, since I was well and free from anxiety about my mother, I would with all my strength devote myself to the care and cure of those many who needed me.

'Hey! Let's have some food! Let's boil some rice!' I cried.

I hadn't eaten anything since morning except for the piece of cucumber. Yesterday's supper had been my last meal. I was sure the in-patients hadn't eaten anything either, for they had been about to take their chopsticks in their hands and begin breakfast when the A-bomb exploded – *Bang!* The staff also hadn't eaten anything because they usually ate breakfast after the patients were finished. Fragments of plaster and broken glass had got into the bowls and pans of rice and miso soup which had been boiled that morning, so more soup had to be made.

For a time it had threatened to rain, but now the sky was clearing little by little. It was just after four o'clock, although I felt as if a month had passed since the morning. We began building an oven, using some loose bricks from one of the shattered walls around the yard. Several of the nurses and the women with mild cases of TB, boiled rice in an iron pot and made some miso soup containing pieces of pumpkin. They also made rice-balls containing pickled plums.

Though the hospital continued to burn, the kitchen and the store-room containing our food supplies had not yet been affected; they were in a semi-basement. But the thick, concrete ceiling of this underground kitchen gradually became quite hot. On the floor above it there was the library where the fire now had a hold. Should the kitchen chance to burn down, our food would all be destroyed.

Brother Iwanaga was absorbed in fire-fighting in the library.

'Joseph!' I called to him. 'Come and have something to eat. You'll feel fitter if you do. You can deal with the fire afterwards.'

Although I called to him, he still went on fighting his way into the burning library, carrying a bucket of water on his shoulder.

In the yard I went round supplying the patients with food, rice-balls and miso soup; and not only the in-patients, but also the injured refugees from the town below – workers from the ordnance factory, those who seemed to be students, and neighbours whose homes had been destroyed. We had a strange sort of picnic, eating unpolished rice-balls and miso soup, watching the hospital burn and hearing the wounded complaining and crying out. Brother Iwanaga; Mr Noguchi and Mr Matsuda, both seminarians; Miss Murai and Miss Oogushi, both nurses; Mr Kawano; Mr Ueki, Mr Matsuzaki and Miss Mine, in-patients who had mild cases of TB and were now helping to care for the other patients and distributing boiled rice – all of them took a leading part in this picnic and gathered around in a circle.

'It tastes very good! It's very nice!' Mr Noguchi enthused. He was twenty-two and came from Omura.

We also drank some tea.

Now I began to recognize the degrees of injury sustained by the staff – the bruising on the face of Father Ishikawa, the cuts caused by broken glass in the face of Dr Yoshioka, the fractured leg of sixteen-year-old Miss Murata, who was in charge of the kitchens, the ugly contusion on Mr Yamano's leg, the cuts and bruises of the chief nurse and Brother Shirahama, and Miss Toshiko Kataoka's injured shoulder; she was sixteen and one of our three young probationer nurses. Brother Shirahama was still suffering from shock, and lay in a coma.

We had carried out all the in-patients between us, including the serious cases, and only two of them had been injured by flying glass.

'Nobody's been killed!'

'Wonderful, wonderful! Everybody's safe!'

'Seventy in-patients, and none badly injured nor burnt to death!'

The hospital, the X-ray machines and 10,000 volumes of books on religion and medicine were all, however, among the flames. Everything, down to the nurses' belongings and mine, was burning, for we had been too busy carrying out the patients to see to any personal effects.

I said over and over: 'What does it matter if these things are burnt? Who cares about the machines and building? Everyone's safe! Everyone is alive!' I repeated this many times, as if trying to persuade both myself and all the others.

Our supper party came to an end with each of us feeling quite emotional. Shadows began to lengthen as the day drew towards a close. Now we had to improvise some beds for the in-patients and those who were seriously wounded. Even when the hospital was fully equipped and all the doctors and nurses on call, just one patient admitted with serious burns or with some external injury or a fractured thigh-bone, would have had all the staff bustling about. Now our situation was dire indeed: smoke continued to pour out of the building; all our medicines and instruments had been burnt or destroyed. Moreover, apart from the in-patients lying about the yard and needing attention, there were other survivors, some with serious burns, some with fractured bones, some with their faces badly cut.

What am I to do? I wondered. In fact, I felt totally at a loss, for I was not so fit and not too strong myself, and my strength was waning fast.

But I raised my voice and said: 'Let's carry the rice-bags out of the gymnasium and use that as a sick-room!'

Not far from the main hospital building was a barn-like building, facing the yard, which had once been used as a gymnasium by the students of the theological school and was now being used as a rice store-house by the Nagasaki Food Corporation. It occurred to me that if we cleared all the bags of rice away we could tend the patients there. Two nurses, some theological students and a few mild cases of TB were, however, all that could be spared to help me, and as I soon grew tired, the work made little progress. Besides, my name was being called out on every side. It became obvious we couldn't possibly remove all the straw rice-bags from the gymnasium. My idea was useless – we would never be able to clear the building before nightfall.

In the meantime, I returned to Dr Yoshioka, who still lay among the trees beyond the stream, on the verge of dying through loss of blood. I re-bandaged her face, tightly. She seemed all the more pitiful since she was a woman, and worse than that because she had been wounded in the face. We decided to try to carry her back. Brother Iwanaga and Mr Noguchi carried her turn and turn about on their shoulders, back to the hospital.

I also saw Mr Kinoshita – he had turned black and was gasping. Mr Kawano carried him to the hospital on his back, crossing the little river and staggering up the path. Mrs Kinoshita followed behind, plodding hopelessly along with her baby on her back and sobbing. We also had to carry Mr Tsujimoto, as well as his wife. He had been lying by the river, his flesh now burnt black. Brother Iwanaga and Mr Kawano bore him on their backs in turn, but he was too heavy for either of them. His daughter and brother-in-law went and fetched a sliding door from the ruins of Motohara town. Brother Iwanaga and Yoshimi Noguchi helped to carry Mr Tsujimoto on the sliding door, struggling up the narrow path to the hospital. How dreadfully different he was, this groaning, agonized man; a shadow of the man I had met early that morning! We also carried his wife to the hospital on the sliding door.

While we were thus employed the dusk of evening began to descend. It was then that my father unexpectedly appeared. When the bomb exploded, he had been working as usual at the law courts in the business centre of Nagasaki city, south of the epicentre. He had rushed out of the building, thinking that a bomb had fallen on the court-house. The destruction thereabouts was not so extensive. No houses had been destroyed. There was a rumour that the bomb had been dropped in the area between Nagasaki Station and the Urakami district. He made his way towards the hospital, anxious about his wife and son. Near the station he found his route blocked by raging flames. So he made a detour through Tateyama, to the top of Kompira hill. From there he was astounded to see twelve square kilometres of the city ablaze. The Urakami district in particular presented a truly terrifying sight, which at once convinced him I must be dead. He was rooted to the spot with horror. Eventually, pulling himself together, he descended the hill. The smoke became thicker, the smell of burning filled the air. People staggered up to him, injured by flying debris, by glass, by fire.

'What's been hit?' he wanted to know. 'Has Urakami Hospital been damaged?'

'Help, help me!' It was all they said.

As he approached Urakami, the seriously injured increased in number and the smell of burning became a stench. He thought there was little chance that his son and his wife could have survived. He saw that the hospital was on fire. He thought his last duty would be to search for their remains. Steeling himself to do so, he managed at last to climb the hill and reach the hospital, six hours after the explosion.

'Oh, you're not hurt!' he said to me, his eyes becoming dim

45

with tears; delight welled up in his throat. 'Now I've found my son and my wife alive and well, I ask no more!'

At the hospital he was shocked to see Mr and Mrs Tsujimoto, with whom he had talked that morning when they were in the best of health. Now they were charred and moaning in pain.

Mr Tsujimoto's eldest son, Yokichi, came in great haste to the hospital as dusk began to fall. His strong features grew pale at what he saw. He had been in Fukuoka at eleven o'clock that morning. As soon as he heard on the radio that a new bomb had been dropped on Nagasaki, he hurried to the station and caught a train going south. He had to leave the train at Michinoo, two stations to the north of Nagasaki Station. Those whose homes were in Nagasaki and those who were anxious about friends and relatives who lived there left the train in a panic. Seeing strange-looking injured people, crowds of refugees, a man who was crazily searching for his family, people smelling of smoke or burning timbers, Yokichi thought: Something terrible must have happened. He walked on and on in great unease. When he rounded a hill and looked down at the area between Sumiyoshi and Ohashi, he was astounded. He hurried on along the railway track between the burning buildings, the dark clouds of smoke, and the injured who hurried past him helter-skelter. The very sleepers he trod on smoked and burned. How was it that even the sleepers could burn, he wondered. Passing through the sea of smoke, he was seized with fear. He saw that the whole area of Okamachi, in which his family lived, had been reduced to ashes. He realized that his wife and all his children must have died. There was nothing he could do for them. He set out for Motohara town where his parents lived. When he got to Urakami Hospital, he discovered his ageing parents, who used to be so strong and robust, changed almost beyond recognition.

We carried Mr and Mrs Tsujimoto into the store-house and laid them down in a corner among the rice-bags. In the dark, dusty store-house we placed Yokichi's cinder-burnt parents. He knew very well that we had no treatment to give them. But he asked me: 'Don't you have *any* medicine?'

I answered: 'The hospital has been entirely destroyed, I'll . . . tomorrow morning I'll . . .'

Mr Kinoshita was brought in and laid alongside the Tsujimotos. Yokichi sat down beside his parents and gave them some water. It was all he could do. But even the water was polluted. We couldn't use the water from the well because it was full of debris. In the end, all we could do was pray.

Mr Tsujimoto and Mr Kinoshita were Catholics. Since they were Catholics, they prayed to Mary with all their hearts. They prayed to Jesus, Mary and Joseph. 'Blessed be Mary, full of grace . . .'

Mr Kinoshita said to me: 'Prayer is all we have left to us. What else can help us now?'

Although I was a Buddhist, I understood.

As it was cold on the concrete floor of the store-house, Mr Noguchi laid a mat in the patients' bathroom in the basement and placed Dr Yoshioka there. It was the only part of the hospital that had escaped from being damaged by the blast. As dusk fell, Dr Yoshioka's old mother as well as her eldest brother arrived at the hospital from the family home in Nishiyama. The mother had walked over the mountain pass from Nishiyama, seen a sea of flames and smoke below her and, fearful for the safety of her beloved, precious daughter, had hurried on down through the crowds of severely injured people who moved up the slope towards her. At last she reached the hospital. Dr Yoshioka's mother was well over seventy years old. She was a very courageous woman. She saw her daughter bandaged all over the face but alive.

'You have done nobly,' said her brother. 'You fell at your post. Be of good courage.' So her brother spoke to her. It seemed to me as if he were talking to himself.

I murmured softly: 'I'm responsible for her injuries.'

But she was in good hands. The chief nurse, Miss Fukahori, as well as Miss Murai, Miss Oogushi and Miss Kajimoto from Takahara Hospital, tended her one after the other. Her old mother and her eldest brother remained at her side.

Happily, none of the in-patients had been scorched by the blast or burned in the hospital fire, for at eleven o'clock, when the A-bomb exploded, it was breakfast-time, and all of them were indoors. This relieved my worries a little, except that there were three seriously-ill tubercular patients, two of them injured by flying glass, and a woman patient who was slightly deranged. The rest were patients who were able to look after themselves.

I went among them. 'Everyone – wrap yourselves up in

anything there is and sleep wherever you can tonight. I'll see what I can do for you tomorrow.'

I spoke loudly, and the patients replied: 'We haven't any mattresses.'

I felt abashed and said: 'I'm sorry about that. Sorry.' Some of the patients laughed.

As it happened, when the A-bomb exploded various patients had run out of the building, some taking personal belongings and clothes with them. Some of these had carried their mattresses on their shoulders. At the time I had shouted at them: 'Don't take your clothes and mattresses with you! It's dangerous. Leave them alone!' I had been thinking of how, during recent fire-bomb air-raids, people carrying such burdens on their backs had been set alight by sparks from the fires. 'Put them down!' I had shouted. 'Run! It's more than enough to escape alive. Save your lives!'

The patients who did as I told them now didn't have any mattresses. The patients who hadn't listened to what I said were able to sleep in comparative comfort.

'Doctor, I need a mattress!' said one patient, making fun of me.

I scratched my head and said: 'I'm very sorry.'

We were regaining some sanity.

By now, night had fallen. It had been a long, long day. Down in the city the red of raging fires was reflected against the smoke. The Mitsubishi Steel Works was burning brightly.

One of the patients said: 'There's a coal depot in the steel works – it must have caught fire. It will go on burning for days.'

By the glow of the flames, in the burning city, we could see in silhouette the ruins of several large buildings – Chinzei Gakuin Secondary School, Shiroyama Primary School, Yamazato Primary School. It seemed that the western side of the town was also on fire.

Someone said: 'Thousands of rice-bags are stored there under the ground. They must be on fire. All that rice is burning.'

'Oh, what a waste!' said somebody else.

The families of two of the in-patients, Mr Fukushima and Mr Murakawa, came to the hospital from Nakagawa town and Narutaki town to take their sons home. Both sets of parents were overjoyed to find their sons safe and sound. Apparently the fire had not spread as far as the districts of Nakagawa and Narutaki. They cried: 'Thank you, thank you very much, doctor and nurses!' After many expressions of gratitude, they left happily for their homes with their sons. I felt a little easier in my mind, for I had handed over two of my patients to their families. But most of the rest had to sleep out of doors. In the dark night sky there was still the occasional sound of enemy planes, and their distant lights flew high above our heads like shooting stars.

By now the hospital fire had nearly burnt itself out. But the library still glowed red in the darkness like a fireplace. Brother Iwanaga had tirelessly gone on pouring water on the burning books, more than a hundred times carrying a bucket of water on his shoulders into the blazing room. The library had contained thousands of books about Catholicism, religion and philosophy, written in Latin, French and Japanese. I couldn't bear the sight of these innumerable volumes being burnt to ashes. Others had helped Brother Iwanaga from time to time, but soon became tired out. He persisted, however, afraid that the beams in the floor of the library would be burnt through and that the fire would spread to the adjacent dining room, to the store-house of food and the kitchen in the basement below. For a time, in fact, the kitchen and the dining room were as hot as any oven.

I heard a voice in the dark hospital yard. 'Doctor, won't you come and have some *sake* with us?'

I flung myself down on the grass, exhausted.

Mr Noguchi produced a bottle of *sake*, saying: 'I managed to find this in a corner of the kitchen.'

He, one of the other patients, Mr Ueki, and I drank the *sake* from a rice bowl as we sprawled on some grass in the yard.

'It tastes wonderful!' I said.

Indeed, after such a long period of continuous strain, this bowl of rationed-out *sake* was a tonic pervading our exhausted bodies and nerves. We had nothing else to talk about.

'Oh, that's nice! That's good!' we said.

Near us the little boy whom Mr Kawano had brought from the burning city was still crying: 'Mummy – drinky! Mummy!' He continually called for water and milk. Other voices called out, echoing around the hospital, the voices of those who were searching for lost persons – 'Tanaka!' – 'Mitsuru!' The only road to the town was now the one which ran down in front of the hospital between Urakami and Nishiyama. Countless refugees and the injured trailed up it, passing the hospital, fleeing from the city. In the other direction went people from Nishiyama, going down to Urakami all through the night, searching for their sons and daughters who as students had been mobilized as members of the volunteer corps in factories and schools. They came into the hospital yard, calling the names of those they had lost. 'Hallo! Is So-and-So there of Such-and-Such school?' It seemed as if they hoped to summon their lost ones out of the bushes, or out of the fields, or from the banks of the stream, from wherever they had taken refuge and lain down to die.

My brother-in-law, Sakuju Takenaka, appeared unexpectedly before me in the dark. He was the chief pharmacist in Nagasaki Teishin Hospital to the south of the city.

'Tatsu-chan,' he said. 'Have you seen my wife? Has she come here?'

'No, she hasn't,' I replied, unmoved.

'Dear God!' he said. 'Suzuko must have been killed! She left home about ten o'clock this morning on her way to visit you. She must have been bombed on her way here!' He sat down on the grass with his head in his hands.

I said: 'She may indeed have been killed.'

I took the news of my eldest sister's probable fate quite calmly. Compared with my delight in finding both my parents alive, my sorrow for the death of one member of the family seemed much less.

'Very well,' murmured my brother-in-law. 'I'll go back and look for her.'

He summoned up all his resolve and left the hospital in search of his wife. For four days he was to search for her without sleep or rest, but he would never even be able to find her corpse. My sister, who was 36, was probably passing through the epicentre at the moment of the explosion. She must have been incinerated in a second by the incandescent flash, together with tens of thousands of other men and women, at 11.02 a.m.

'Come on,' I said to the others around me. 'Let's get some sleep. We'll have to sleep in the open tonight.'

I lay down among those who were as worn out as me in a corner of the hospital yard, furthest away from the main building. All I had was a blanket.

I said in a scolding tone: 'Get some sleep now! Go to sleep!'

Yet few were able to sleep that night, least of all those in Nagasaki city.

Someone, calling out loudly, passed by in the dark: 'Mr Mitsubishi – Mitsubishi! Answer if you are there!'

Another voice spoke: 'Doctor, please examine my husband.'

Mrs Kinoshita stood before me, her child still on her back. She said: 'I know you are tired, but . . .' She came for me several times. 'Excuse me,' she whispered. 'My husband is in pain.' She woke me up every hour.

'Doctor,' said the chief nurse. 'Please don't go any more – you'll break down if you do.' She was related to Mr Kinoshita but she was anxious about my health. She tried to prevent my going. I was certainly sleepy and tired – I didn't feel like getting up. But Mrs Kinoshita stood over me, sobbing in the dark. I told myself: Even if I go to see him, I can do nothing for him.

But weakly I got up and went to where he was lying. His condition was deteriorating by the hour. Old Mr and Mrs Tsujimoto were next to him, both still moaning. Their eldest son, Yokichi, was in constant attendance upon them.

At about midnight, Mr Tsujimoto's condition suddenly worsened. I was called again to the storehouse.

'Can't you do anything?' asked Yokichi.

'Tomorrow I will get hold of some stimulants for his heart and some pain-killers,' I answered wearily.

But even if I could get hold of such medicines, I thought, what use would they be to someone so severely burnt?

By degrees, Mr Tsujimoto's breathing became harsher. I couldn't feel any pulse. I just stood there beside him in silence. Brother Iwanaga, Mr Noguchi and Mr Matsuda, Miss Fukahori and Miss Murai, all gathered about him. They prayed to Jesus, Mary and Joseph. They asked that his soul be received in heaven. They besought the help of Jesus, Mary and Joseph in the last moments of his life. The prayers, which had been spoken softly, gathered in volume, becoming louder and louder. The voice of Brother Iwanaga was loudest of all. Suddenly Mr Tsujimoto went into a violent fit of convulsions; his eyes bulged.

'His last moment has come!' said someone.

Yokichi burst into tears. It was the first and last time that I would see the manly Yokichi cry. He couldn't bear to watch while his father suffered and died without receiving any treatment. I chanted a Buddhist prayer: *'Namu Amida-butsu'*. It meant much the same as 'Our Father which art in heaven'. Yokichi wept and wailed as if his heart would break.

This sorrowful scene, however, was only one of tens of thousands of similar scenes that night in Nagasaki, and would be like tens of thousands of other woeful occasions which would plague thereafter the people of the city. Those who had someone to cry for them, those who were able to die surrounded by prayer – such persons, in my opinion, died a happy death.

Mr Kinoshita had been seriously burnt, but he still lived, perhaps because he was young. His voice alone now sounded from his sick-bed in the store-house: 'Jesus . . . Mary . . . Joseph . . . Hear my prayers.'

I went into the yard again, to sleep on the grass. It was already midnight. It seemed some creature far away was moaning confusedly. It might have been the lament of the people or the voice of the devil. Other voices went on calling: 'Hello? Mr Sekiguchi? Are you there?' The voices on the road below the hospital continued throughout the night.

I fell asleep with the members of my staff in a corner of the anguished hospital. But none of the people who worked there or any of the in-patients had died.

Many thousands had already died in the city below. About 30,000 died in the first few minutes that followed the explosion, and three times as many would die in the days, the months and the years to come. 'Fat Man' exploded 500 metres above 171 Matsuyama town in the Urakami valley. The Urakami Branch of Nagasaki Prison, 100 metres north of the epicentre and situated on a bluff, was annihilated, as were 134 prisoners and warders. Five hundred metres to the east, about twenty priests and 200 people, come to confession that morning, died in the collapse of Urakami Church. Of about 1,500 children and teachers at Shiroyama Primary School, 500 metres west of the epicentre, about 1,310 died. Almost as many, about 1,300, died at Yamazato Primary School. Shiroyama School had been commandeered in part for use by Mitsubishi war-workers, accountants and others; 138 of them died, out of 157. The pupils and nuns who died in Josei Girls' School numbered 212. Other schools near the epicentre each lost between 140 and 220 children and staff. Over 1,000 doctors, nurses, students and patients died in and around the flaming ruins of Nagasaki College Hospital and the Medical College, out of the 1,800 who were there; 530 medical students died and over 200 patients. Out of 1,720 people working in the Mitsubishi Steel Works, 700 metres to 1·3 kilometres south of the epicentre, 1,019 died. To the north, more than 2,250 died out of the 10,000 in the ordnance factory. Near the steel works, in Sawai town and 1·6 kilometres south of the epicentre, was a prisoner-of-war camp (Fukuoka POW Camp No. 14), in which 169 men were incarcerated: 129 being Dutch and Indonesian, 24 Australian and 16 British and American. Seven of these prisoners were also killed by the bomb.

About 3 per cent of those who died were military personnel; 13 per cent worked in war industries; 84 per cent were ordinary people, mainly the elderly, women and girls, students and children.

On Tinian, General Farrell sent a coded top secret message to General Groves in Washington: 'Strike and accompanying planes have returned to Tinian . . . After listening to accounts, one gets the impression of a supremely tough job carried out with determination, sound judgment and great skill . . . Weaker men could not have done this job . . .'

2

The first day after the A-bomb was dropped on Nagasaki dawned in the hospital yard. The child, brought in by Mr Kawano, had continued to cry all night: 'Mummy! Mummy, drinky . . .' The chief nurse had given the little boy some water and looked after him as if he were her own child.

'Get up, come on, let's get up now,' I said.

As day broke, it grew brighter all around us. The doctors, the two theological students, the few nurses, who had slept in rows out in the open, slowly got to their feet. The sky was cloudless. It looked as if it would be another hot day. The incidents of yesterday seemed like a dream, a nightmare. It was difficult to believe that our whole world had changed overnight. But, in Japan, we have a certain expression which, roughly translated, means that the blue ocean can turn into a mulberry field – that the world is a scene of sudden changes. I remembered the story of the last days of Pompeii, of which I had heard in my childhood, and thought of the people and the city of Pompeii buried under the ashes and lava after Mount Vesuvius erupted.

I gathered up the remnants of my resolution and strength, though I still felt very tired and much depressed. Urakami Hospital had been gutted by fire, though its concrete skeleton still stood; all the medical instruments and medicines within had been reduced to ashes; all my own books and notebooks on medicine, cherished over many years, had also been destroyed.

But there remained nearly seventy in-patients to be cared for; probably few had any homes to which they could now return. Mr Kinoshita and Mrs Tsujimoto still lay severely burnt on the floor of the store-house. Dr Yoshioka had been injured in the face, and Father Ishikawa was badly hurt. Although my medicines, instruments and medical books were all destroyed, I was still a doctor. As long as my body remained sound and I was able to continue my ministrations I remained, and must continue to be, a doctor. The people were in agony. I had promised them that I would cure them somehow or other tomorrow. But how? Parts of the city were still ablaze. Indeed, it seemed as if the whole of Nagasaki had been burnt to the ground. Turning towards the town, I saw black smoke rising into the sky from the Mitsubishi Steel Works and from Urakami Church, and the trees on the hills around us still smouldered.

'Hello, good morning! Did you sleep well?'

I spoke to everyone cheerfully. I went to the store-house and greeted the patients there. But I thought: What on earth am I going to do about treating all these sick and injured people? To tell the truth, my strongest impulse was to run away as soon as I saw the crowd of invalids and the injured. I felt personally responsible for the destruction of all the medicines and medical instruments. Their loss hung over me like a nightmare.

Miss Murai, who wasn't injured, together with some of the other nurses and the three kitchen-workers, set about making a meal. Nobody and nothing moved down in the city, just smoke and flames. It seemed to have died. But soon, in the middle of the hospital yard, smoke began to rise from the makeshift kitchen range we had made of brick.

Then Mr Noguchi called to me: 'Doctor, come over here, please.'

He took me to an underground passage near the kitchen, which had served as a store-house for food and coal and as an air-raid shelter. As soon as I entered the hot air stifled me. Debris still smouldered in the rooms overhead like ashes in a stove.

'It's so hot!' I gasped. 'Is it safe?'

Timidly I followed Mr Noguchi into the underground shelter. He proudly pointed at a recess, and behold – there stood two large and shabby wooden boxes.

'Medicine! But how . . . ? I can't believe it!'

I was ecstatic as I hugged him. He must have had a sixth sense, for he had been storing medicine, little by little, in the air-raid shelter over a period of several days. I was overjoyed; I thanked him repeatedly as I pulled the two boxes out of the overheated shelter. Then, restraining my excitement, I opened them. First of all gauze and bandages appeared. Those on the top had been damaged by water but those below were clean. Then out came some pain-killers, some antiseptic and disinfectant lotions and ointments: Anaesthesin, chloramine and mercurochrome – useful, but quite inadequate in quantity. They could only have been about one hundredth of all the medical supplies in Urakami Hospital and one millionth of all the medical supplies destroyed in Nagasaki city. Their quantities were pitifully small; but, with the gauze and mercurochrome in my hands, my spirits soared.

At 8 a.m. on 10 August I set about treating the sick and injured outside the still-smouldering ruins of Urakami Hospital. Miraculously, all our in-patients had survived. I wasn't a Catholic, but I began my first examinations with a heart full of thanks to God, with something like a prayer, though with only a pathetic supply of medicine.

The day before I had promised to cure Mr Konishita, who lay in agony in the store-house among the straw bags of rice. I sprinkled Anaesthesin over the burns on his face, and also over those covering his shoulders and chest, and laid a gauze on top of them. They covered nearly half of his body and were ulcerated and black; the pain made it difficult for him to breathe.

His wife asked me piteously: 'Doctor, will he be all right?'

'Yes,' I replied. 'He's now out of danger. But you'll have to be patient for two or three days.'

Anaesthesin would do no more than reduce his pain and could not heal such wounds. But when I saw his wife so overwhelmed with sorrow, I could only answer her in terms of hope.

Next I treated the burns of Mrs Tsujimoto, who was lying next to him. She was sixty. Strange to say, her face as well as her back and the rear of her lower legs had been burned. What had happened was this: on hearing the sound of aeroplane engines before the flash, she turned her face towards the sky, her body still bent as she weeded the rice field, and that was how she was standing when the bomb exploded.

I treated her burns in the same way as I had treated those of Mr Kinoshita, with a lotion of Anaesthesin on some gauze. She kept silent in her agony. Her husband had died in great pain during the night. His body was now being buried. On account of her severe burns, she was unable to attend the burial of her husband, with whom she had lived as man and wife for many years. She was more distressed by her grief at her husband's death and by his burial than by the pain of her own burns.

'How do you feel?' I asked. 'Do you feel any better?'

But she only moaned – she was perhaps praying to the Virgin Mary.

As a doctor, I knew that if burns covered less than one third of the whole skin area, then a person's life could be saved. This was what I had been taught, and I depended on this dictum being true. But the real truth was that such burns as these were so extensive they were beyond anything in my experience. These burns were so severe that it would take a long time to treat them. Large supplies of medicaments would also be needed. Even though I had so far treated only two persons, the treatment had been as complex and as difficult as if I had treated twenty out-patients on any ordinary day.

All at once an elderly woman came up to me breathlessly and said: 'Doctor, please – you *must* come and see my injured husband! My house is just below the hospital, about fifty metres away.'

Leaving the many untreated patients in the hospital, I went out with her to visit her injured husband, a nurse accompanying me. For the first time since the day before, I left the hospital and looked down at the panorama of factories and houses below the hospital. There was nothing which had not been gutted, wrecked or reduced to ashes; the buildings with which I was so familiar were nowhere to be seen. There was no sign of any movement, of either man or woman or beast. Electricity poles leaned to one side or else had fallen; trees had been torn up by the roots, their branches broken, and had turned into leafless skeletons in a single night. The town was dead. But where had all its people gone? I believed they also must have all died.

I couldn't even make out the road. Walls on each side of it had been demolished; stone walls or fences around houses had been torn down. I hadn't the slightest idea which house was which. Here and there torn patches of white shirts or mattresses and the remains of scorched clothing were scattered about; some pieces were suspended from electricity wires and poles. Far below and beyond, where columns of smoke still rose from the city, iron skeletons of smashed buildings dotted the wasteland – the signatures of a gigantic devil millions of times stronger than man.

Surely, I thought, coming to what had once been a familiar location, this can't be Mr Tsujimoto's house. Behind a stone wall lay a man protected from the sun by some pieces of plywood. He said: 'I was working in the ordnance factory . . . the explosion injured me somehow . . . my chest.' He spoke in a thin voice.

I examined him and found that he wasn't seriously wounded, but he seemed very weak and feeble.

Another old woman, a stick in her hand, her hair awry, came up the slope towards me, crying – 'Hey!' Seeing who I was, she pleaded: 'Help me, doctor, I beg you!'

It was the mother of the man who was lying on our store-house floor, old Mrs Kinoshita.

Her husband's spacious shop and his home had been totally wrecked. Among the pillars and planks and debris a little patch of boarded floor remained, and Mr Isematsu Kinoshita lay there with a wound in his head. When the bomb exploded he was working in the rice fields. He managed to avoid being directly exposed to the flash since, on hearing the plane, he promptly hid behind a stone wall and fortunately escaped from being burned. But the blast threw him on to the ground. In his head he sustained a cut about five centimetres long.

'You're very lucky,' I told him. 'Yours is only a slight wound.'

I tried to console him, but he was very apathetic, covering his bruised and bloody face with his hands and not saying a word. He was a kindly, respected man, a member of Urakami Church. He had been a landlord and his business had done well. I wondered: Has he lost all his will-power because of this sudden change in his fortunes? Has he been weakened by the wound in his head? It wasn't so. He was anxious about two of his children – a son, who lay in Urakami Hospital, dying in agony from the burns which covered his body, and a daughter, a teacher at Shiroyama Primary School; she was still missing.

He whispered: 'She's probably dead.'

His eldest son was in the services and far away; the wife of that son had been severely injured. His eldest daughter was married to Mr Yamagami, who lived just down the road. He asked me to inquire after the Yamagamis – and I walked on down the hill.

Mr Yamagami's house on the hill of Motohara was in an even more wretched state. The previous morning he had been working as usual at the Mitsubishi Ordnance Factory. When the explosion happened, he was inside the reinforced-concrete building of the main office-block. He realized immediately that something dreadful had happened when a great blow struck the building. Heedless of the cuts and bruises which he got when he was flung across the floor, he dashed outside. As large and as strongly built as the factory was, it caught fire in an instant. Men and women rushed about like so many wounded animals. Mr Yamagami hastened towards the hill of Motohara, worried about his family, his heart ready to break at the sight of burning houses on his way there. But he managed to return home safely, only to find his own house ablaze and all but levelled to the ground. Happily, however, four of his children had been rescued by his wife, although the fifth had been crushed and killed by a falling beam.

Mrs Yamagami had been trimming potato runners in the sweet-potato fields. In the explosion she had been seriously burnt like many others, on the face, the back and on both her upper arms. But, disregarding her burns, she had hurried home, anxious about the house and her children. She found the house on fire but not yet totally ablaze. Even as the fire spread, she scrambled among the wreckage, overturning the roof-tiles and lifting fallen timbers with her bare hands, striving madly until she had rescued the four surviving children from the ruins and sustaining more burns in the process. From the roasted fingers of both her hands, which had pushed aside red-hot roof-tiles, peeped the exposed bones.

The whole family was now lying in an air-raid shelter.

Mr Yamagami said: 'I'm so happy that these at least are safe!' He added, 'My eldest son, who's a member of the volunteer

59

corps at the middle school, hasn't come home yet. But four of my children at least have escaped with only a cut or two.'

In spite of their anxiety at the fate of their eldest son and their grief at the loss of the child crushed in the ruins, there was still joy in the midst of their pain. But no one could know how this was only the beginning of great misery. As ten days passed, and then another ten days, the four surviving children, one after the other, began to die.

As I walked further down the road with the nurse and approached the first section of Motohara town, the extent of the devastation caused by the bomb became much clearer. It was a dead suburb, wholly burnt, where not a living soul was to be seen. Now and then we heard the unnerving droning of enemy planes in the sky. Each time we heard the sound of engines, the nurse and I took refuge behind something or other. Immediately in front of us, smoke could still be seen rising from Urakami Church. Both of its great Romanesque domes had been torn down. The church had once been the centre of worship for 10,000 Catholics in Nagasaki. Its brick walls now reared from the smoke like broken wooden stakes. Elsewhere, the iron frame-work of a factory roof was bent and crushed as if it had been made of straw. As I went further down, both men and buildings became more and more dreadfully disfigured. An indescribable smell hung over everything. What appeared to be a man's corpse could as well have been that of a beast.

I returned to the hospital, hungry and dead tired. The in-patients, squatting or lying in the yard or in the store-house, regarded me stonily. Their eyes asked: What is to become of *us*?

I examined the in-patients in silence. One patient, named Hayashi, already seriously ill with tuberculosis, had been injured by a piece of glass in his throat. He seemed to be in great pain, and was wheezing. I couldn't make out whether this was due to tubercular phlegm or because the piece of glass had penetrated his wind-pipe. As for the others, four or five had been slightly wounded by pieces of flying glass, more than I had thought. Two or three of them came up to me and asked to be treated. On examining them, I found that their injuries were not too serious.

'There's no need to fuss about such a little injury!' I said. 'You're not badly hurt. A great many people have been much more seriously injured, some fatally – they haven't had any treatment!' My voice rose loudly.

The patients gazed at me reproachfully. As a doctor, I was sharply aware that, however relatively slight their injuries or their suffering, they must for them be very serious matters.

While Mr Kawano, Brother Iwanaga and Mr Noguchi also ventured out of the hospital to see the destruction, I examined those refugees who had been seriously injured and who lay in basement passages or out in the yard. As I did so, Dr Yoshioka's brother said to me: 'Please could you have a look at that young man over there? He's been there since yesterday and needs some urgent attention.'

A young man lay in a concrete corridor. I had often passed him by since yesterday, but had never paused to examine him or given him any consideration. So it was that many a human life ended without any care. How many people, I wondered, had been left lying in the fields or on the roads, without having been given even a drop of water for twenty-four hours or more?

This young man was another student from Nagasaki Medical College. In his case, the A-bomb had exploded during a lecture given by Mr Yasuno, an assistant professor of pathology. He was able to remember Mr Yasuno crying out: 'Lie down!' He had fought his way frantically out of the ruins and run until he reached our hospital.

He said: 'There were about a hundred students in the room – but none of them, except five or six, managed to get out.'

He was very concerned about Mr Yasuno and his fellow students. He himself couldn't so much as move, on account of a blow on the head. I said to myself: His skull must have been fractured.

A large number of such students found their way to the hospital before they died. They had left their homes and were studying at the medical college or working in the ordnance factory as members of the volunteer corps of students. Many breathed their last in fields or ditches, without being given any water or any attention. Most of them died in the course of twenty-four hours, though none had been burnt. All I could suppose at that stage was that their heads or chests had been struck or injured by some falling or flying object. It never occurred to me that the new bomb produced a radioactive fall-out which attacked the inner cells of the human body.

There was little I could do for the young man and I went outside.

In the midst of all this hopeless ruin there was just a tiny breath of renewed life in the hospital that morning. Brother Iwanaga was already considering how to rebuild the chapel and worrying about the acquisition of food supplies. I myself had begun doing what I could as a doctor, using only Anaesthesin and mercurochrome on gauze. Mr Kawano was assisting us in treating the patients and looking after them. Miss Murai and other members of the staff were busy distributing boiled rice with the ever-cheerful kitchen girls. Twice a day, at 11 a.m. and at 5 p.m., they boiled unpolished rice and cooked a brew of miso soup made from pumpkins or wakame seaweed. They distributed rice-balls, not only to the in-patients, but also to the staff, to the people who had managed to reach the hospital yard before collapsing, as well as to our neighbours.

Mr Takeuchi, chairman of the local residents' association, came to the hospital.

He said: 'I feel a little bit better, more able to cope, after coming here. This rice tastes very good.'

He took a big mouthful of boiled unpolished rice which we were all sharing. He had been chairman of the residents' association of the second section of Motohara town for twenty years. His second son had been a student at the theological school run by the monastery of St Francis, but he had given up his schooling because of the war and was now a soldier, fighting at the front. Mr Takeuchi's neighbourhood had been completely destroyed, all the families injured and their houses broken or burnt. His third son had also been badly burnt.

He said: 'Your nurses have quite a job on their hands – distributing boiled rice and looking after the patients!'

So saying, he went away.

One thing had been worrying me all morning: whether or not the family of Miss Fukahori, the chief nurse, was safe. She came from Motohara town, and her family – her old mother and her brothers – lived near Urakami Roman Catholic Church. Her eldest brother was the owner of a factory and her second eldest brother was an engineer in the Mitsubishi Shipyard. They were a happy, well-to-do family. She must have been deeply concerned about her mother's safety since the A-bomb explosion the day before. All day yesterday the town had been a sea of fire, and her mother must at least have been in considerable peril. But Miss Fukahori said nothing about her anxieties, and continued to care for the little boy brought in by Mr Kawano, giving him water and a little porridge. No one dared speak to her, either about the child or her mother.

During the morning Brother Iwanaga and Mr Noguchi went down into the town without telling the chief nurse about their intention to search for her mother, in the expectation that the most they would find would be her corpse. Meanwhile, Mr Kinoshita the younger had been removed from the hospital store-house and taken home, his severe burns still untended. During the afternoon his wife came looking for me again. Once more she stood before me, her baby on her back, in tears.

I went with her back to the Kinoshita home, afraid that he would at last be nearing his end. The sun was beginning to set. From his ruined home came the voice of his old mother, praying: 'Jesus . . . Mary . . . Joseph . . .'

I examined him where he lay on the only clear patch of floorboards among the wreckage; his aged parents stood beside him. His breathing was harsh and irregular; the pupils of his eyes were dilated. Although his young, strong body had endured the pain of his severe burns ever since the explosion, his life appeared to be drawing to its inevitable close.

His wife asked: 'Is there nothing we can do?'

I shook my head. My expression was answer enough.

His old mother began praying more loudly. 'Jesus! Mary! Joseph!' she cried. His injured old father bowed his bandaged head, as if in prayer.

With the sobbing of the wife and the praying of the mother pursuing me, I walked back along the road as dusk began to gather. I was so depressed in spirit, overcome by the grief and pain of human existence in this transient world, that I felt as if I were myself insensible, lifeless, like a ghost.

It grew dark. One by one Mr Kawano, Brother Iwanaga and Mr Noguchi returned to the hospital. Bit by bit they described the devastation in Nagasaki. We had now given up any hope of getting any medical supplies or surgical equipment. The raging flames in the city streets had spread beyond Sakaya town, east of the city centre.

I talked with Mr Kawano. I said: 'Takahara Hospital and Kuwasaki Hospital may have been saved from the flames. I hope so. If so, we'll be able to borrow some supplies and instruments from them.'

'No you won't,' he said. 'Remember, almost all of their supplies were removed to this hospital some time ago for safety.'

We looked at the hospital and felt all the more gloomy to see it blackened and still smoking. Down in the city the Mitsubishi Steel Works continued to burn, a dull glow in the night sky.

'The coal depot must still be burning,' I said. 'I wonder when the fire there will be put out?'

'Dead bodies are also burning,' said Mr Noguchi. He looked drawn and very tired. He continued: 'We couldn't get near Urakami Church – nor could we reach the home of Miss Fukahori's mother. The river was jammed with corpses ... I heard that a medical team from Omura came as far as Motohara hill, but they didn't stay long.'

'How I envy them, that they can leave when they like!' I exclaimed. 'We can't. We're stuck here!' I felt angry and abandoned.

He said: 'They probably turned away in horror, seeing such heaps of the dead. Would you like some *sake*?'

Each of us drank a cup of *sake* in the dark.

Mr Watanabe and Mr Sonoda, who were in-patients, were called for by their families. Finding their sons safe and sound in the ruined hospital, their relatives cried and wept for joy.

'You're very fortunate,' I said as I saw them off.

Those who were delighted that their relatives lived, those who grieved about those who had died, those who still didn't know whether or not their families had survived – all were enveloped by the deep night of 10 August.

In the hospital, we settled to sleep once more in the grassy yard. We slept out under the sky, each wrapped in a blanket. The droning of enemy planes could be heard above us now and then; cold shivers ran through us from head to toe. The badly injured, hearing that sound, shuddered, fearing that they would be bombed again and maybe killed.

*

At dawn the little boy brought in by Mr Kawano died. All night long he had gone on crying: 'Mummy, mummy.' Miss Fukahori stayed with him all the time, tending him, but in vain. He was baptized before he died. Now he was able to join his mother, who had already died and who waited for him in heaven.

Brother Shirahama, who had been in a coma most of the day before, began to recover. Father Ishikawa's face had swollen and was now black and blue; it was a pathetic sight, seeing him lie prostrate on a blanket in the bare yard.

Outside the yard, in the sweet-potato fields, lay the blackened body of a middle-aged man. He must have managed to reach the hospital during the night before collapsing and dying where he fell.

I felt disheartened at the mere thought of trying to treat so many patients and injured people with only a handful of medicines. As it became lighter, crowds of wounded people came staggering up to our hospital, where they thought there must be doctors.

Near the rear gate, in a corner of the hospital yard, a clinic was established, though it didn't deserve the name. A sheet of cloth was stretched over four supports, fashioned from a big bamboo stick brought by the parent of one of the wounded. Mr Noguchi had rescued some desks and chairs which had formerly been used by the students; somehow they had escaped being burnt. So it was that something like a field-hospital was set up, equipped with the barest essentials, with the minimum of medicines, bandages and gauzes. Mr Kawano and I took charge of the treatment. The nurses helped us, but they also had to take care of the distribution of boiled unpolished rice and miso soup.

Brother Iwanaga, Mr Noguchi and Mr Matsuda began to set up a makeshift chapel inside the hospital, where all the fires had at last been extinguished, after much difficulty. Luckily, the staff dining-room next to the library remained more or less undamaged. Brother Iwanaga began to reorganize it as a chapel; but it had been blackened with smoke and smelt of burning and seemed just like an oven.

During the morning three children were brought to me by Brother Iwanaga, along with their mother. The children had been badly injured in the head; so had she. The mother was half-mad, raving like an idiot; her eyes were vacant and she was deeply shocked. Her eldest child, thirteen years old, had a raw wound in his skull that was big enough to take my fist. I could do nothing for them. Each wound was too serious to be dealt with by the usual surgical treatment. Besides, stitching any wound without the necessary equipment was out of the question.

About noon, a soldier, wearing the arm-band of a military policeman, apparently a sergeant, happened to pass the yard. When he saw me treating the patients in twos and threes, he cried out: 'Why aren't you doing something for all these other people?'

He took me by surprise – I didn't know what to say. I said: 'I'm doing what I can – as much as I can.'

He shouted at me again: 'Can't you do anything for all these people passing up and down outside the hospital?'

I was much provoked at being upbraided by this man for my unavoidable incapabilities. I shouted back at him: 'This hospital has also been bombed! We have no medicines or medical instruments!'

He turned away in silence. How dare he say such a thing, I thought. I muttered to myself behind his back: It's you, you soldiers, who have brought this misery on us. Give us back what we had.

I felt bitterly resentful. For a time I was very upset.

Then Mr Takeuchi, chairman of the residents' association, called on us again at lunch-time. Eating rice-balls with us at the entrance of the basement air-raid shelter, he said: 'Doctor, I hear that the Japanese air force have also dropped this new bomb on the American mainland – and that we have recaptured Okinawa and Attu Island, Kiska and Saipan. They've all been bombed, and our combined fleet has set out on some auspicious mission.'

He talked excitedly. Despite the fact that his neighbourhood had been destroyed and his own house demolished, he seemed to be extraordinarily cheerful. It seems men will lose their hold on reality in any last extremity. It has been said that a man dying of thirst in a desert will smile at the thought of an oasis. Mr Takeuchi's smile was just such a smile in certain respects.

I said, laughing at his delusions: 'How can that be true? It isn't at all likely.'

But he firmly believed a Japanese atomic bomb had been

dropped on New York and Washington. I snapped back at him: 'I'm fed up with that kind of story! Even if it were true – that the Japanese air force had dropped such a bomb on the Americans – I would never rejoice, I swear it. Haven't enough people been killed or injured? Haven't enough lives been lost?'

I could no longer endure the thought of all the useless, reciprocal killing and wounding. Mr Takeuchi went home again.

That afternoon, several nuns, teachers at the Josei Girls' School, each terribly lacerated, were brought to the hospital on stretchers. The school, run by the Junior Jesus Society, stood near Urakami Church. When the A-bomb exploded, the school building was destroyed in an instant and caught fire, and a number of the pupils and sisters were killed, including the principal.

One of the sisters, seriously wounded, said with a smile, though breathing with difficulty: 'I have been saved through the mercy of the blessed Virgin Mary.' She thanked me and the nurses for treating her wounds and whispered: 'It's a mercy that you and the nurses weren't injured. That's something like a miracle. Our Lord is merciful – he has left alive those who are now needed the most.'

I never thought for a moment that Jesus had left me alive because I would be needed. But, strangely enough, as chance had fallen out, I had not been hurt. Some would say it was a miracle. I was therefore all the more determined to save the life of this innocent girl who had devoted herself to Christ.

During the afternoon I visited several of the injured where they lay in their homes. Mr Kawano also went out on his rounds and walked down-town. Brother Iwanaga and Mr Noguchi walked as far as Urakami Church. This time they found Miss Fukahori's mother in an air-raid shelter. She was alive and appeared not to have been harmed.

To begin with, I visited Mr Tsujimoto's family. I treated Mrs Tsujimoto's burns. She was dying in agony. There was nothing I could do to ease her pain. She had not strength enough to recover from her burns; soon she would be dead. Her son, Yokichi, had gone to Oka town to look for the remains of his five children. Yesterday he had buried his father's corpse. Today he gathered the scorched bones of five of his children. Later he had to prepare for his mother's burial. He endured his sorrows with great fortitude, behaving like a man, with dignity, ever praying to God. He set off for the graveyard on the hill with a hoe on his shoulder, followed by his younger sister and his youngest son, who were happily left alive. The sight of his broad shoulders, somewhat bowed, sank deeply into my mind.

I visited the wrecked shop and house of the Kinoshitas. Young Mr Kinoshita's dead body had been left where it lay. His father was still in pain from his injured head.

In the air-raid shelter of the house, I discovered several injured people, among them Mr Yamano, who had been pinned under a fallen tree in the yard of Urakami Hospital.

'I can't stand up – I feel dizzy,' he complained, breathing feebly. 'I feel sick in my stomach, and everything tastes bitter.'

'But you haven't been injured, have you?' I said encouragingly.

'I don't think so,' he said. 'But I can't stand up.'

'It's because you've been staying in the air-raid shelter. Get outside and take a breath of fresh air. You'll soon feel better, I assure you.'

I knew nothing as yet of radioactivity and neutron rays. But among those with no burns at all were many who felt sick in their stomachs and had a burning sensation in their mouths. I thought it was because they had stayed inside shelters ever since the bomb was dropped. Yet, as time passed, they began to suffer from bloody diarrhoea and bleeding gums, followed by bleeding under the skin. The interiors of their mouths turned purple. This was how it was with Mr Yamano.

'I'm afraid it must be dysentery,' I said.

I felt a chill, gloomy foreboding. I knew how dysentery could become rife on battlefields or in devastated areas. If it's dysentery, I thought, it could be very serious. In fact, it was far worse than dysentery, but I couldn't have known that then. No, none of us could have known how terrible their sickness really was.

I visited Mr Yamagami. I learned that two of his six brothers had been killed. One of them had joined the volunteer corps and never returned. The other had been killed on the spot when he was crushed by a falling beam. His four surviving brothers had been only slightly injured, and we remarked on how fortunate they were. But this feeling of relief was, to tell the truth, destined to be only a passing reassurance and joy, as many families would find. Those who felt secure because they had only been slightly wounded, or not wounded at all, were to die one by one as ten days passed, and then twenty days. Each was to fall victim to the invisible, evil power of the bomb.

A few days after the bomb had been dropped, those who were close to the epicentre and yet were lucky enough to have been only slightly injured, those who were buried under ruined houses and yet amazingly escaped unhurt, or those who happened to be behind some obstruction or other and escaped being burnt, all remained fit and well. I now felt I understood the limits of the new bomb's destructive powers. I went so far as to think that if, at the moment of explosion, we could cut off the heat rays with some screen or shield and somehow avoid being crushed by collapsing houses, we would remain alive and well. This belief was not merely due to ignorance and simplicity. Even the leading scientists of those days had no more knowledge or experience about the new bomb than we had.

After sunset that day I read a copy of the newspaper *Asahi*, which Mr Masahichi Kawano brought to the hospital from town. It was the first time I had seen any newsprint since the day of the explosion. I pored over the crumpled paper as if I had just returned to the civilized world after two or three days in hell. It said: 'Announcement from the Ministry of Home Affairs – there is the possibility of getting burnt – be sure to take refuge in an air-raid shelter – there's no better refuge against the new bomb.'

According to an on-the-spot report, the new kind of bomb used by the enemy on Hiroshima had been dropped hanging from something like a parachute; the explosion had made a great noise; the power of the blast was huge; it gave off intense heat; it caused damage over a considerable area. But, the paper said, if you paid attention to the points which followed, damage and injury could be reduced to a minimum. These points were apparently quite effective, and had to be put into practice.

1. Don't relax your guard even in the case of a single enemy plane. When a large one appears, you had better take shelter, even if it is on its own.
2. Taking refuge in an air-raid shelter is a very effective measure. Don't remain outside aimlessly.
3. You should choose an air-raid shelter with a roof. If it has no

roof, go outside and cover yourself with a blanket or some clothing.

4. When you are caught out of doors, you must reduce the exposed part of your body because any exposed parts may be burned.

5. When you take refuge in a shelter, be careful of leaving anything behind that will cause a fire in your kitchen. There are many examples of fires that have started in houses that have collapsed.

That was what the *Asahi* said. We already knew more about what could happen than that, through bitter experience.

What was the use of a blanket or some clothing when everything would be burnt or charred in the brilliant heat of thousands of degrees Centigrade? What opportunity did we have to go outside after putting out our kitchen fires when, in an instant, tens of thousands of homes became tinder-dry and burst into flames? Professor Nishina and several top Japanese scientists had received a warning, issued by a group of American scientists. They must have known about the dreadful destructive power of the new bomb – and, what was more terrible, about the devilish power within it which could invade the core of every human being. But there was nothing about any of this in the newspaper. As families shed tears, clasped each other by the hand, overjoyed at finding each other only slightly hurt and free from burns, top American scientists were convinced that no life could possibly exist at the epicentre for seventy-five years to come.

Of all this I knew nothing whatsoever. I would continue to visit my patients with straw sandals on my feet. Brother Iwanaga and Mr Noguchi would walk down to the city, to Urakami Church. The nurses would go on working in the hospital yard.

Among the patients I called on were the Mr Yamada and the Mr Mizoguchi, whom Mr Kawano had visited the day before. Both were master carpenters and were being cared for in an air-raid shelter by their families. They had been building a shelter for the sisters of Josei Girls' School, and had completed most of the work on it when the bomb exploded. It was flattened like a matchbox. Both Mr Yamada and Mr Mizoguchi lay unconscious for some time under the fallen timbers. A large splinter of wood had buried itself in Mr Yamada's thigh, and another had been embedded in Mr Mizoguchi's scalp. They lay there all that day, but on the following day managed to reach their houses in Motohara town, crawling on their hands and knees. It was nothing short of a miracle that they were able to reach their ruined homes; their families cried for joy.

I extracted the piece of wood from Mr Yamada's thigh, leaving a gap big enough to swallow my fist. I bandaged the wound with gauze after dabbing it with dark red mercurochrome. Fortunately, I was able to stop the bleeding. Mr Mizoguchi had also been badly injured as I found when I inspected his head-wound. His skull had been fractured; his hair was matted with blood. I examined the wound with a pincette, and felt something hard. I pulled out what I thought was a splinter of wood, but it turned out to be a piece of periosteum from the upper cranium. He fell intermittently into a coma. He died before the end of the month.

Treating them was very tiring and I wished I would never have to deal with people in such a state again. I felt utterly depressed and helpless. Inside the shelter, however, were ten other wounded people. It was stuffy in there, and smelt abominably. These people complained of nausea and headaches.

I shouted at them: 'You ought to get outside! You're rotting away in here!'

The droning of enemy planes could be heard from time to time, and on each occasion they set children in the shelter crying.

Stooping uncomfortably over the injured, I spent half a day in that air-raid shelter treating the wounded, only returning to the hospital after sunset.

Everyone was waiting for me. Brother Iwanaga and Mr Noguchi, who had gone into the town again, reported how far the city had been devastated. I was told that large fires, which had broken out simultaneously in the Urakami district, had burnt down everything as far as Goto town, on the other side of Nagasaki Station; while the fire which had started at the prefectural office had spread as far as Sakaya town before it stopped. Half of Nagasaki city had been destroyed.

A first-aid station had been established at Yamazato Primary School, but had been closed after only one day. No one knew why. I thought: With all the injured who've gathered at the hospital, I will never be able to close this wretched first-aid station. I couldn't help feeling resentful – there was no chance of me running away.

During the day, several fire-fighters and volunteer guards had arrived from neighbouring villages to help us deal with the dead and injured. A large number of the injured were carried in open freight-cars from a makeshift station between Michinoo Station and Ohashi to the national hospitals in Omura, Isahaya, Kawatana and Ureshino. The dead were gathered in heaps here and there, ready for cremation. I grieved for the charred and wounded people who were loaded on to flat carts as if they were fish in a market, and separated from each other; wife from husband, parent from child.

When night fell, bright new flames could be seen near the steel works, where bodies were being cremated. As we gazed at those distant specks of light we shared our scanty supper in the darkness of the yard. It was our third night there.

Then suddenly, in the pitch dark beyond the yard, there was a hum of voices. It seemed that there had been some new arrival. In a moment my ear caught the dear voice of my former teacher, Dr Takahara, who had laboured with me in establishing the hospital on Motohara Hill. Although I had last seen him earlier that week, it seemed as if we had not met together for years: everything had changed so much, the people, the city and the hospital. He came towards me, saying how sorry he was for his late arrival. He was accompanied by two nurses. I said: 'Everything in the hospital has been destroyed, as you can see – the X-ray machines as well. I'm sorry. But not a single in-patient has been killed. We've managed to save them all!' It was still our only consolation.

Dr Takahara, who was fifty-nine, appeared to have been greatly shocked by what he had seen on his journey. He had visited Urakami and a number of other districts and had seen for himself the appalling wide-spread destruction. He met Dr Yoshioka, whose face was heavily bandaged, and apologized again in a tearful voice for being so slow in coming to the hospital. He cried out when he saw the chief nurse, Miss Fukahori, asleep on the ground. Finally, he wept when he found the in-patients, all of whom he knew by sight, lying huddled together on the floor of the store-house. At last he gave way to the grief he had so far managed to control after his journey through the hell on earth into which Nagasaki had been transformed.

'We Japanese never knew till now the full horror of war.' So saying, Dr Takahara, who was born in the Meiji era, wept.

That night, he shared the hardships of the staff and the in-patients; he was loth to leave us and return to his own hospital. Under the stars of heaven, he slept with us in the yard.

Two nights before this, in the early hours of 10 August, the six members of the Japanese War Cabinet – Premier Suzuki, aged eighty-one, the Foreign Minister, Mr Togo, the Navy Minister, Admiral Yonai, the War Minister, General Anami, the Army Chief of Staff, General Umezu, and the Navy Chief of Staff, Admiral Toyada – had met in an underground shelter in Tokyo to discuss the situation after the Russian invasion of Manchuria and the A-bomb attacks. The 124th Emperor of Japan, descendant of the Sun Goddess, a small, nervous, introverted man, bespectacled and with a high-pitched voice, presided. Aged forty-four, he had ruled Japan for eighteen years, his reign having been named by him at its start as Showa, Peace. Suzuki, Togo and Yonai were in favour of surrender; Anami, Umezu and Toyada against. They all made speeches, airing their views on the Potsdam Declaration and the state of the nation. The A-bomb disasters were hardly mentioned. They had no clear idea of casualties and knew nothing of fall-out and radiation sickness. They knew that many more people had died in the Tokyo air-raid in March and that as many had died in other cities, of which sixty-six had so far been bombed. The atomic bomb was just another bomb, albeit very large and immensely destructive. The Cabinet disagreed 50-50 about what to do. Then the Emperor spoke. He said: 'Continuing the war can only mean destruction for the nation and a prolongation of bloodshed . . . I cannot bear to see my innocent people struggle any longer. Ending the war is the only way to restore world peace and to relieve the nation from the terrible distress with which it is burdened.'

Later that day, a message was transmitted directly to Washington, saying the Japanese government were 'ready to accept the terms enumerated in the Joint Declaration', provided the declaration did not include any demands which prejudiced 'the preroga-

tives of His Majesty as a sovereign ruler'. The Americans consulted their allies and began drafting a reply.

In Tokyo, on 11 August, fifteen senior army officers met to plan a coup d'état. *In Fukuoka, a hundred miles north of Nagasaki, other army officers butchered eight captured American airmen. That night, just before 1 a.m. on 12 August, America's reply was radioed to Japan from San Francisco. It reaffirmed and elaborated the Potsdam Declaration. Concerning the Emperor, it said: 'From the moment of surrender, the authority of the Emperor and the Japanese government to rule the state shall be subject to the Supreme Commander of the Allied Powers . . .' This reply was discussed at a full meeting of the Japanese Cabinet at 3 p.m. Meanwhile, General Umezu and Admiral Toyada had been pressurized by the younger army officers into visiting the Emperor and urging him to reject the American response. General Anami was also buttonholed by senior officers seeking his outspoken support for a military* coup. *The cabinet meeting was adjourned until an official communication from all the Allies was received.*

3

Everything and everyone was now in a wretched state. The people and the hospital had changed so much that even Dr Takahara, a Buddhist, had been moved to tears. But next day the sun rose as usual. We glanced reproachfully at it, at the way it rose as serenely as if nothing untoward had happened. All the people at the hospital had spent the night in the open. Wearily and sadly they saw another day begin. It was Sunday, 12 August.

'It will be hot today, like yesterday.'

We each began to think about what we must do in the hours ahead. Dr Takahara and I conversed together for a while.

'Victory in war always meant everything to the Japanese,' he said. 'We never thought of the misery of defeat.' He talked as if Japan was already defeated. Eventually he realized he had to return to his own hospital. He said: 'I'm so glad that all of you are safe. I could wish for nothing better than that nobody here has been killed. Nothing is better than being alive. While there is life, there is hope.'

He repeated his words to the staff and the in-patients of Urakami Hospital. It seemed he was only repeating what he had so often been telling himself.

He spoke about his brother. He said: 'My brother returned to us safely yesterday. When the bomb exploded he was at the rear of the Mitsubishi Ordnance Factory and escaped being burnt.

After spending the night there, he reached Yagami unharmed. He's a lucky boy.'

But, a week later, his only brother was to die a sudden death, leaving six children behind. Dr Takahara as yet knew no more than the rest of us how the scourge of Satan, radioactivity, flayed people from within.

After Dr Takahara had left, Mr Kawano and I plucked up courage and began the morning's surgery. The Anaesthesin, mercurochrome and gauze that we had depended on were running short. Mr Kawano went into the city to search for some more drugs and medical supplies. 'The college hospital has been entirely wrecked,' he said. 'I'll have to go somewhere else and get what I can.' Brother Iwanaga and Mr Noguchi were both occupied with setting up the chapel in the dining room.

More and more patients came to our clinic, mainly from the area of Urakami Church. Most had been only slightly injured. But their gums were bleeding, as were their bowels. Most of them explained their symptoms in the same way: 'I'm losing blood like this because I must have breathed in some poisonous gas.' They all said they felt sick in their stomachs. There were dark red specks of blood in their mucus membrane and under their skin. I wondered if they were being caused by dysentery or purpura. None of these people had been burnt, as they had happened to be protected by something or other when the bomb exploded. These signs were, in fact, the first physical symptoms of radiation sickness.

I went back once more to the Kinoshitas' shop. Their daughter, a teacher at Shiroyama Primary School, had returned home three days after the explosion, covered with dirt, panting for breath, her back cut by flying glass. I examined her. Fifty, sixty – no, uncountable numbers of pieces of glass, one centimetre or two in length, had pierced the skin all over her back and penetrated the muscles. I seized a piece of glass with a pincette. I tried to pull it out, but failed. By pulling on it strongly I managed to extract a sliver of glass, but the rest was deeply embedded. I had never seen an alien substance penetrate muscle so deeply.

At eleven o'clock on the morning of the explosion, she had been sitting in the staff-room of Shiroyama Primary School, with her back towards the windows. The school stood on a hill. The immense pressure of the A-bomb blast struck the windows almost horizontally, shattering the window-panes, and at the same time, hurtling the pieces against her back with such force that the fragments sliced through her thin summer blouse and buried themselves in her body. Their velocity must have been about 200 metres a second. The destructive force of the A-bomb blast was far beyond our imaginings.

I applied mercurochrome to each glass cut, and then pulled out the piece of glass within. After pulling a piece out, I used mercurochrome again to disinfect the cut. It took some time to extract the pieces and as I pulled them out, each time she gave a scream of pain. When the fragments had eaten too deep into her back, I had to make an incision with a surgeon's knife, a rather dull one, and then draw out the glass therein. At last she asked me to stop, complaining of her pain, weariness and weakness. I also felt exhausted. I had managed to extract ten pieces at the most. The rest were innumerable – her back was pierced all over with fragments of glass.

'I'll get the rest out tomorrow,' I said and stood up.

Walking downhill away from the house, I wondered how deeply those pieces of glass had actually penetrated – perhaps as far as the vertebrae or the lungs. It was too cruel.

Mr Takeuchi, chairman of the residents' association, appeared once again at the hospital, as I sat in the yard and ate some boiled unpolished rice.

'I hear that Urakami Hospital's to become an official first-aid hospital,' he said, though I was very doubtful about the origin of such a report.

Many of the injured had by now been taken from Ohashi and Sumiyoshi to Isahaya and Omura. A day-hospital had been set up in the ruins of Yamazato Primary School. But, in air-raid shelters all over Motohara town, thousands of the injured still lay without having received any kind of medical treatment. It was a serious problem.

'Well,' I replied, 'it's a good idea. A first-aid hospital ought to be set up in this neighbourhood. If this building hadn't been burnt down, it would have served the purpose well enough. But only look at it.'

I gazed despairingly at the black and ruined hospital, which seemed like a grinning skull.

I said to Mr Takeuchi: 'When is some relief party going to get to us? Aren't we going to get any medical supplies from the army or the navy?'

But he knew nothing about any of that.

Shortly after noon, a civilian patrol arrived at the hospital. Its leaders were two assistant police inspectors. The patrol consisted of about thirty people, most of whom came from the Kawanami Shipyard on the edge of the harbour. Mr Takeuchi was with them.

'We are here by order of the authorities to open a first-aid hospital,' said their leader gravely, in a manner becoming his position.

I was poor-looking and small, and my navy-blue suit was moreover stained with mercurochrome, blood and dirt. Who would have thought that such a figure could be the doctor in charge?

'Where is the well?' one of the leaders enquired.

In Urakami Hospital there had once been a large well with a good supply of water. But now it was useless because, when the A-bomb exploded, the bricks of a chimney had fallen from the roof and down the shaft. As a result we had decided to make use of an indoor well, which yielded a much smaller supply of water. Up till then I had rationed its use. The water from this indoor well had so far sustained the lives of the in-patients, the staff and about a hundred refugees. The civilian patrol now began drawing water freely from the well.

I protested nervously: 'The water of this well is all we have, so please be sparing with it.'

At lunchtime, the patrol leader asked me to provide his men with some food. It was more in the nature of an order than a request.

I protested again: 'We've also been bombed and made homeless. Besides, the nurses are very busy distributing boiled rice to the patients in addition to their normal duties. We haven't time to make meals for you as well.'

It was the leaders of our nation who had begun this ruinous

78

war, and as a result the ordinary people had suffered most severely. The mere sight of an officer or a policeman made me irrationally angry. But they paid no attention to me.

In addition to the thirty members of the patrol, more than a hundred others now arrived as reinforcements, volunteers from the Kawanami Industry Company. They were divided into two groups.

The first group entered the hospital ruins and began to put the first floor in order. The floors of the first and second storeys were made of solid concrete, fifty centimetres thick, and had remained in one piece. The whole of the first floor was a jumble of burnt panelling, plasterboard, beams, broken bits of furniture, cupboards, tables, chairs, medicine cabinets, machines, all manner of bottles, and so on; some of the glass and metal had melted. Stretchers were made from two poles and a straw mat and the blackened debris was carried out on them by the volunteers.

The second group also constructed some stretchers, and these went down into Motohara town. After a while they came back, carrying whatever injured people they could find. From the air-raid shelters in Motohara town these other volunteers brought up the wounded who had still received no attention. A tally was kept of each man or woman who was brought into the hospital; some I knew, despite their burns. 'Ninety, ninety-one . . .' the count continued. I was appalled to see how many people had hidden away in the shelters.

The number of patients we received now rose above 150, each of them seriously injured, whether suffering from fractures, cuts or burns. Some of them smiled at me with joy, in expectation of the treatment they thought they were now going to receive.

Towards three o'clock, when nearly 200 patients had been brought to the hospital, one of the volunteers, standing at attention, informed the group leader that their work was finished.

He answered: 'Thank you very much.'

I went up to him and demanded: 'Who's to take charge of this first-aid hospital? Where will the medicines come from?'

The group leader whispered in the ear of one of his men, who dashed outside. After a while he returned and said something to his commander, who then stated that I was to take charge.

I refused flatly, saying: 'I'm the only doctor here! What can I do with so many patients by myself? I have no medicines, no instruments. This is a war-damaged area and I'm the doctor of a war-damaged hospital. I can't take charge of all these people!'

I hadn't yet been able to treat even my own in-patients and the staff. How was I going to get food for all of them? How would we live?

The leader said: 'You're a doctor, aren't you? Very well then. Since you are a doctor, you'll have to look after them. Do your best.'

I said: 'If this hospital hadn't been burnt down and the medical supplies and equipment with it, I would have been able to care for them. Most of them I know, and even if I hadn't been asked by you, I would have done my best for them. As it is, I have no medicine.'

One of the patrol was sent outside, and about twenty minutes later returned with some supplies.

'There you are,' said the group leader. 'This will have to do. Good-bye.' Leaving a parcel of medical supplies behind them, they went on their way.

It was four o'clock in the afternoon. There was just this one parcel of medicines. With a nurse I opened it up. Inside were some bandages, fifty gauzes, some sanitary cotton, a pound of zinc oxide oil, some tincture of iodine, alcohol and a few candles. It was less than a day's supply. The person who had brought us these supplies had no real knowledge of what was required.

The patrol had departed, having done what they intended to do – setting up a first-aid hospital in just one day – leaving me behind with a bit of zinc oxide oil and a bottle of iodine among a great crowd of patients who had been seriously burnt or injured and were endlessly moaning and in pain.

Wretchedly I surveyed the ruined rooms, still littered with fire debris and each as hot as an oven. All the windows had been blown out; the ceilings were black; the rooms were choked with charred debris, with fallen stones, bricks and lime, which the patrol had heaped high in each corner, leaving a space in the centre of each floor. Not much debris had in fact been carted away. They had brought in large quantities of straw from neighbouring farms and scattered it on the floors. Upon the straw more than 200 severely wounded people now lay – no, it looked more as if they had been simply thrown down. Five or six members of one family, all of whom I knew by sight, were

(a)

(b)

(a) The plutonium bomb 'Fat Man'
(b) The mushroom cloud that rose
over Nagasaki when 'Fat Man'
exploded, photographed from
one of the observer planes.

Urakami Hospital

Urakami Catholic Church

Josei Girls' School

train heading north from Urakami Station

Nagasaki before the war

Urakami Hospital

Urakami Catholic Church

Josei Girls' School

Yamazato Primary School

railway line X

Mr Takami's tennis court, the epicentre of the bomb blast

After the bomb had dropped. The same scene, some months after the bomb had dropped.

Mitsubishi Ordnance Factory

Urakami Prison

epicentre

Yamazato Primary School

Urakami Hospital

Josei Girls' School

Urakami Catholic Church

Nagasaki after the bomb had dropped, looking north-east

(a) Ruins of Mitsubishi Steel Works
(b) Streetcar destroyed approximately 1,000 metres from the epicentre

(a) House wrecked by the blast, about 2,000 metres from the epicentre.
(b) Shadow of a washing line on a wooden wall, approximately 3,000 metres from the epicentre.

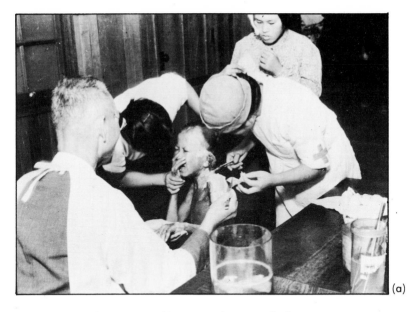

(a) A young boy being treated for severe burns at Shinkozen Primary School, a temporary first-aid hospital

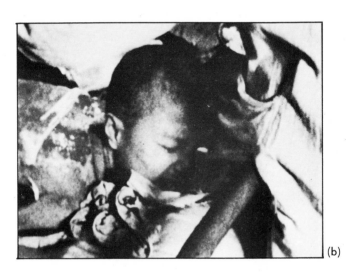

(b) Sixteen-year-old Sumiteru Taniguchi was cycling away from the blast 1,800 metres from the epicentre when the bomb fell. The back of his body was severely burnt and he had to lie on his front for one year and nine months in hospital — he eventually survived.

Dr Akizuki at St Francis Hospital, Nagasaki, June 1980

seriously injured. Those who had been only slightly hurt tried to comfort their more severely injured companions and relatives, who were groaning in agony and crying out for help.

By five o'clock, there was still no sign of the start of any treatment. The groans and lamentations of the injured echoed loudly in the ruined rooms. With the help of a nurse, I began to provide such treatment as I could as it began to get dark. Inside the hospital it was already twilight. Miss Mine held a candle for me. The candle's light swayed as the wind blew in from the openings in the windowless walls. The light veered on the edge of extinction.

I spread zinc oxide oil over a burn. I soaked the tip of a writing-brush in the oil and then spread it over the inflamed surface of the burn, which was extensive, reaching from the waist as far as the neck and face. How was it that both the skin on the face and that on the back had been burned at the same time? It was because the victim, working with his back to the sun, had turned his face to the sky on hearing a plane – and just then the A-bomb flashed. When I spread zinc oxide on these burns, the victims screamed; *'Ah! Awh, awh, awh!'* The whole process took a very long time. In the case of those whose injuries had been caused by flying glass and wood splinters – and how terrible some of these were – I disinfected the wound with mercuro-chrome or iodine, extracted the alien substance, and then covered the wound with a gauze. This took even longer. Each injury was so severe that, even in peacetime, it would have taken fully two hours to treat such a patient individually, and the operating theatre, the instruments and clothing would have all been stained with blood. Now I had to treat such patients one by one and on my own and with almost no facilities.

Far overhead, the engine roar of an enemy plane could still be heard from time to time. Both the slightly hurt and the seriously injured would again be seized with fear and cry out: 'Put out the light!'

I stopped what I was doing, extinguished the candle and waited for the plane to fly away before setting to work again.

Three hours had passed since the patrol departed. I had not yet treated even ten of the new patients. Nearly 200 were still waiting to receive attention. Children cried to their mothers for help. People called out: 'Doctor, it *hurts*! Quick, oh come here quickly!'

In the swaying candle light, the black figures of the injured writhed on the shadowed floor like so many wounded beasts.

I carried on with my endless work in anger, despair and silence. The wounded complained bitterly at being treated by me alone. Children waited, weary with waiting, and because they were exhausted. I was also very tired – it was hard to keep my eyes open. It was now ten o'clock at night. The endless task of spreading zinc oxide oil on burns continued in the dark.

'Isn't there anyone else – any assistant doctor?' voices demanded. 'Can't we get any help from the army or navy?'

I felt bitter about the patrol who had departed, leaving so many helpless and injured people at the hospital.

'I'll go to some army or navy hospital for help,' I said, standing up angrily. 'Tomorrow.' But neither I nor the survivors of Motohara knew that the Japanese army and navy had already been all but annihilated. I said: 'I can't do anything more for you today. The rest will have to wait until tomorrow.'

I abandoned the patients. I couldn't go on. The untreated patients cried: 'Doctor, are you going to leave us? Have pity! Please help us! Do something to help us!'

However loud they cried, I could do nothing more. My strength had gone. When I returned, exhausted, to the yard, I found Miss Murai, Mr Noguchi, the chief nurse and the in-patients all waiting for me, anxious about my health. They spoke words of encouragement and comfort.

I lay down and pulled my blanket over my head. Tears poured from my eyes. I wished I could also leave this place, just as the patrol had done, even if it meant abandoning the wretched survivors. I hated myself and wept tears of self-pity. I knew I couldn't leave.

It was no easy matter getting up the next morning, partly because of the discomfort of camping out every night, and partly because I felt so depressed, as if lead were lying in my stomach, remembering that nearly 200 people had been brought into the hospital the day before.

My intention now was to escape into the country with my

parents, as soon as every hospital patient with tuberculosis had been sent home and everything else had been properly dealt with.

Each day, families had been arriving to claim relatives among the in-patients. About half of the seventy in-patients who had been in the hospital when the bomb dropped had now left, congratulated by all on their good fortune. The thirty or so who remained either came from remote villages or had had their homes damaged. They were mainly engaged in the distribution of rice and in assisting the staff to make the hospital ruins habitable. Those with mild cases of TB worked hard and well, taking no notice of their own illness. Mr Ueki and Miss Mine were particularly useful to the staff. Oddly enough, their health improved. But the condition of the several in-patients who were seriously ill with tuberculosis took a turn for the worse, as it was very hot during the day, and at night they had to sleep in the store-house, which was hard enough for those who were comparatively healthy. Mr Hayashi, who had been injured in the neck, and Miss Kawanishi, who had become psychotic, both deteriorated fast, left on their own in the store-house. I felt sorry, but it couldn't be helped.

'I must get round to seeing them,' I muttered as I ate from a bowlful of boiled rice with the nurses.

Mr Kawano, who had gone into town the night before, had come back with some zinc oxide powder, some sesame oil and more tincture of iodine. That morning, when I went on my rounds, taking my scanty remedies with me, fifty or sixty of the 200 injured people who had been brought to the hospital were no longer found to be there, either because they had felt nervous in the empty, ruined rooms, or because they had been scared by the occasional sound of enemy planes, or because they were disillusioned by the treatment afforded by only one doctor and his bottle of zinc oxide oil. They must have absconded during the night. But over a hundred victims still remained – there was nowhere else for them to go to.

Bracing myself, I began to visit the patients with the untrained Miss Mine, herself an in-patient – the nurses were too busy cooking and distributing meals. There were still many patients lying in the ruined sick-rooms, demanding my attention. I was able to identify quite a few people that morning, although yesterday I hadn't been able to because of the darkness. I discovered that in many cases complete families had been burnt, or that all the children of one family had been seriously injured.

The four children of Mr Yakichi Kataoka had been brought to the hospital. Their burns were extensive, from shoulder to buttock. When I began to spread zinc oxide oil on their burns and sterilized them with mercurochrome, they cried out for their mother, complaining at the sharp pain, and whenever they did so, she hugged them, enveloping them with her concern, like a mother crane sheltering her wounded chicks with her wings. She said: 'How could they injure such little children? They are innocent – they have never harmed anyone.' Her husband, Yakichi, was fighting in some distant war zone. He was a good Catholic and had been a teacher in the theological school before he was sent to the front.

'Let everything be as God wills,' said the Catholics. But it was surely not God's will that these children should have been so badly burnt. They whimpered and cried day after day; and then two of the boys died of tetanus.

More than twenty young women and girls, with severe burns, had been brought in on stretchers from a near-by orphanage run by the sisters of the Convent of the Holy Cross. More than thirty sisters looked after the orphans from their infancy, raising them in the Catholic faith under the motto 'Pray and Help'. At that time there were about forty infants in their care. The sisters' duties were divided: over ten of them looked after the orphans, and ten or so others, young and vigorous, managed the convent's small farm.

At 11 a.m. on 9 August, these young sisters, dressed in black, were weeding in the rice fields. The white flash of the A-bomb scorched and burnt their backs and the backs of their legs. The rice fields were about 500 metres below Urakami Hospital, and consequently the heat-ray and the blast were considerably stronger there. Some of the sisters died within a few days.

The rest now lay on the straw in one of the wrecked wards, cruelly burnt. Those sisters who had been inside the convent, preparing some milk in the nursery, were injured by glass or pieces of wood. The chief nurse, Sister Yamada, was badly injured and died soon afterwards, grieving for the children, most of whom had been killed. The large building that had been the Convent of the Holy Cross was completely destroyed by fire.

These wounded sisters now had nowhere to go. Telling the beads of their rosaries as they lay on the floor, they intoned, 'Happy is gracious Mary,' again and again, trying to ignore their pain. They were watched over by a few frightened elderly sisters and by some of the older orphans, not much more than ten years old, who had, until then, been cared for by their charges. I felt all the more miserable at this terrible transformation of the sisters, having seen them in far different, happier circumstances five or six days ago.

I said, as I spread the zinc oxide oil on their backs: 'Be patient – you've only to keep patient for a week. In a week's time you'll be much better.'

They replied, tears in their eyes, pressing their hands together: 'Thank you, Doctor. You're doing your best.'

I was ashamed of my crude methods of treatment, using only zinc oxide oil and iodine. It was so inferior to the measure of their gratitude. Great advances had been made in the making of the atomic bomb, far beyond human comprehension; weapons and science had far exceeded imagination. Yet here I worked in a most primitive fashion, spreading zinc oxide oil over extensive burns with a writing-brush. Silently I apologized for what I did and had to do.

Apart from the many people among the victims whom I had known before in this neighbourhood, there were many injured who were strangers to me. Among these were volunteer workers from the Mitsubishi Ordnance Factory, members of the home guard, and students from the medical college. Several of the latter, injured on 9 August when the bomb exploded, had fled as far as Motohara, where their strength gave out. They were found later, lying on the ground, and brought to the hospital on stretchers by a relief squad. For several days they had lain in the dirt and their wounds had begun to fester, and become a feast for flies.

At first sight, the gaping wounds on their backs seemed to be packed with something like boiled rice – which proved to be maggots. I picked them out individually with a pincette. The vitality of the grubs was so great that the wounds were seething with them, as if they had been crammed with fistfuls of boiled rice. The patients weren't, however, aware of this since the wounds were on their backs. I picked the grubs out one by one. They kept moving continually and it was difficult getting hold of them. It took a long time. I performed this task over and over again, and Miss Mine and I both began to feel sick.

Treating all the patients on my own was an impossible, endless task. Eventually Mr Kawano came in to help me, and I escaped out into the hospital yard about noon. There I ate a meal that served as both breakfast and lunch.

I was supping a bowl of miso soup with some seaweed in it when I noticed a stern-looking army officer crossing the hospital yard in some haste. As he approached I recognized him. It was Captain Fukahori, a medical officer and a pharmacist at the military hospital in Omura. He had once been the chief pharmacist in Urakami Hospital. His home was in Urakami, and he was a relative of our chief nurse. He was a strong and vigorous man, but his face was wet with tears.

He had walked through the ruins of Urakami, through the heaps of corpses in Urakami of the Christians and their families. Then, after visiting the pitiful ruins of the Kinoshitas' home, he had come to our hospital, where over a hundred people lay in great misery. I took him to the chief nurse, having asked him to say something heartening to her. He went up to her and said: 'Your pain is not only yours but that of the whole country. We must stick it out to the end.'

As Captain Fukahori was an officer at Omura Military Hospital, he must have had some idea of how wretched Japan was and would be after the two atomic bombs had been dropped on Hiroshima and Nagasaki. His words rang hollow, for I remembered, ever since the Manchurian Incident, how boastful his army had been. They would always say how invincible our forces were and how victorious at the front; military announcements were only of brilliant results in battle. What would they say of our misery now? Before we were aware of it, the war had changed into one of survival, into suicide tactics and a scorched-earth policy. I was deeply disillusioned with the army – and even now, one of its officers was ordering people to clench their teeth and stick it out.

All that apart, I knew Captain Fukahori to be a decent man.

He said to me before he left: 'I have to go back – there's much to be done. Please look after my uncle and aunt, Mr and Mrs Kinoshita. And also the chief nurse, Miss Fukahori. I must go.'

I got him to say he would provide us with some more medical supplies. The lack of them was ever in my mind. He hurried away, telling me to send someone to fetch some medicines from Omura. Mr Kawano was kind enough to start for Omura at once.

I noticed at meal times how the flies that came into the yard were becoming a great nuisance. They had increased immoderately over the past few days.

That afternoon, several nurses from Takahara Hospital arrived, carrying a stretcher on which there were no patients but various useful articles – candles, matches, paper lanterns, rice-bowls, paper – sent by Dr Takahara, who was ever attentive to such details.

A report reached me that Miss Fukahori's aged mother had grown worse; yet she had seemed to be not in any danger. A chilly foreboding ran down my spine. A number of people had died in succession over the last few days after developing symptoms which I associated with dysentery and purpura: dark red, purplish spots in the skin, bloody excrement, and loss of hair.

I forced myself to shake off any feeling of gloom and said to Brother Iwanaga and Mr Noguchi: 'She may have got worse because of all the time she spent in that air-raid shelter. I'd like you to bring her to the hospital.'

They hastened down to Motoo town. When I returned from visiting my patients in the neighbourhood the old lady had already been brought in on a stretcher. She had been laid on the concrete floor of the bathroom in the basement. Her daughter, the chief nurse, was weeping on her knees beside her.

Miss Fukahori's mother was seventy-four and dangerously ill. She had great difficulty in breathing. Her skin had blackened, and only the mucus membrane of her mouth was whitish. She had hardly any external injuries. Yet her last moments had come.

'Old Mamma!' The chief nurse broke down, crying over her old mother. I pitied her greatly: she would now be very much alone. More than ten of her relatives had already died. I went outside.

Something I had been most concerned about over these last few days was the fact that I had not yet finished treating the facial wounds of my colleague, Dr Yoshioka. Later on that day, towards evening, I was provided with a stitching-needle and some silk thread through the generosity of Kuwasaki Hospital. Since I had been so careless as to let all the medical equipment in my hospital burn – which had been entrusted to me by Takahara Hospital and Kuwasaki Hospital – I had felt ashamed to ask for any new supplies. But I had been bold enough to ask if I could borrow a stitching-needle and thread.

The sun had set, and it was getting dark. I thought: I must do it now – I must do something about the wounds in her face, without any further delays.

I had Dr Yoshioka and Miss Murata, whose thigh-bone had been fractured, taken and laid on beds in the burnt-out library. For the first time in five days since they were injured, they were laid on beds indoors. From a medical point of view, it was not advisable that an old wound should be stitched, but I was going to defy this dictum. I wondered what her mother, brother and even Dr Yoshioka herself thought about the fact that, for five days, her wounds had been left as they were. I felt very bad about it.

In the dark library, Miss Murai sterilized the stitching-needle, its fittings, and the silk thread, by boiling them in a rice-steamer, in lieu of any sterilizing apparatus. She also sterilized the gauzes by boiling them. I removed the bandages from Dr Yoshioka's face and peeled off the gauze that had stuck to her wounds. I saw that the scars were smaller than I had feared. I stitched up the gash between her eye and the bridge of her nose, then one on her upper lip. The lacerations on her face were so livid that her mother and brother couldn't bear to look. Miss Murai, holding a candle in one hand, with the other picked up the end of the thread, using a pincette; her face was in a sweat. The dull light of the candle flame flickered in the breeze that came through the wide, bare windows.

My hands trembled as I stitched the large cuts in the face of my colleague. I hoped and prayed that the wounds wouldn't fester. At last I finished the suture and, after dressing the cuts with a clean bandage, I felt much better, as if a weight had been taken off my mind.

Strange to say, her injuries never became septic, despite the decrease in her white corpuscles, despite the unfavourable climate of summer and the poor sanitary conditions; but I overlooked the extraction of a piece of glass from her lower jaw – probably because I was so much on edge.

As the library had now been put into some sort of order, seven or eight persons could be accommodated there besides Dr Yoshioka and her family and Miss Murata. Mr Noguchi, Miss Murai and I were now able to stop sleeping out in the open. I covered the floor of the bathroom in the basement with straw mats. This was to be my bedroom from now on, windowless as it was. There would be no more sleeping under the stars.

I began to lose track of how many days had passed since the explosion; the weather continued dry and hot. It was, I think, on 14 August that some indications of life began to be heard in the ghost town which was Motohara.

The survivors' first concern had been to find somewhere to live. Limping out of their air-raid shelters, they had gathered boughs, bits of wood and iron sheeting that were lying about. They propped them against some bank or tree, making a lean-to which would protect them from the night-dew and the scorching sun of day. They were glad they had survived (but did not know how their sufferings were to continue for many days, months and even years as they struggled to stay alive). They began to wander out into the ruined city. Although they had themselves been injured, they felt it was their duty to search for the remains of relatives who had been killed.

They turned over each tile in their wrecked homes, tiles which had been broken into pieces about three centimetres square and were heavily pitted, having been fired in the temperature of thousands of degrees Centigrade. Once these pieces had been pushed aside, they came across layers of wall-plaster or roof-plaster and ash, which they had to burrow through before reaching the charred remains below. Those who were employed in this gruesome task, searching through the ashes, looked like death themselves. Very probably they became contaminated in their grim search through the unseen presence of large quantities of radioactive dust. We eventually called this dust 'death sand'. These people were destined to die before long, but at the time we had no idea of the peril they were in.

For formidable foes to life, radioactivity and disease-bearing bacteria, lay in wait for the survivors. The colossal energy of the new bomb had not only destroyed everything in a flash, it had also sprinkled a fatal dust all over the ground, infecting the earth and also the human body.

Apart from all this, as people slowly took up the threads of their lives again, flies multiplied with a vengeance by day, as did mosquitoes by night; and many bodies lay rotting among the ruins. There were, besides, many animal corpses, cows, horses and dogs. These became infested with maggots, which produced many more flies that bred thousands of others in turn.

Miss Sugako Murai was busily distributing boiled rice. She had to prepare meals for over a hundred persons. A great many radioactive particles must have clung to the pumpkins and egg-apples which had been out in the glowing sun and which we consumed in our miso soup.

Assisted by Mr Kawano, I continued to treat the sick and injured. He visited Omura more than once and each time he brought back medical instruments and supplies and told us how the war and relief work were progressing. Each time he returned he went the rounds of in-patients or visited those who lay outside.

Our monastery hospital, Urakami Hospital, had by now resumed some of its functions and was being relied upon by the local people – even though it was short of everything and badly damaged. It was a great source of pride to me and to Brother Iwanaga: the continuance of the hospital's spiritual role, its medical duties and its daily routine. It seemed a blessing, a gift of God, from the Christian point of view. Where else in the city had so much been achieved within a few days after the explosion? And where else had the bodies and souls of so many people been healed?

Four days after the A-bomb exploded, on Tuesday morning, I visited the rooms where the TB patients were lying on the concrete floor. The two serious cases among them were Miss Kawanishi and Mr Hayashi. Miss Kawanishi's mind had been affected by the air-raid warnings every night, even before the bomb was dropped. After the bomb her mental derangement grew still worse, being aggravated also by bad conditions and hot weather. She was eventually taken away by her elder sister.

Mr Hayashi's mother came to see him from her home in Omura. She was overjoyed to find him still alive in Urakami Hospital – she couldn't believe it. He was seriously ill with tuberculosis, apart from the fact that he had been wounded in the neck, near his throat. Every time he breathed in and out, he wheezed.

His mother repeatedly asked: 'Why is he wheezing so much, Doctor?'

I feared that fragments of glass might have penetrated the trachea, but I could do nothing about it. All I could say to encourage her was: 'It's all right. His injury will heal up soon enough.'

The other patients who had TB were able to look after themselves. But they wanted to know what would become of the hospital, and of them. They looked at me anxiously. I said to myself: How do I know what will become of the hospital when I don't even know what will happen to me tomorrow?

About thirty of the in-patients had nowhere to go. Their homes being in ruins, they continued to live in the wrecked wards of the hospital. In addition, nearly a hundred people injured by the bomb still lay in the ruined rooms on straw or on mattresses brought from air-raid shelters in the vicinity. My most important task was now to do what I could for them.

The sick and the injured continued to call at the shattered porch of the hospital; some were carried on the shoulders of one man, others by several men. I also did what I could for them. Unfamiliar symptoms in sickness and death began to grow in number. One man brought to the hospital was found to be dead on arrival, his skin a dark purplish colour. He came from the area of Urakami Church. As he had appeared to be dying, his neighbours had carried him to the hospital, hoping he could be given some treatment by a doctor – but they were too late. As such cases increased, I began to wonder more and more what parts of the body were being affected and how these deaths were being caused.

The victims of the bomb already in the hospital also began to exhibit a number of gradual and disturbing changes. I repeated the treatment of disinfecting the surfaces of burns with mercurochrome and by spreading zinc oxide all over them. Oil for burns was acknowledged as the most practical method of treatment; it was here being spread thickly over nearly fourth degree burns. Now that nearly a week had passed since the bombing, new and healthy scar tissue should have begun to develop, as would normally have been the case. As it was, the injuries of these patients went through two distinct processes.

In the first, the burns became very dry – in fact they dried up. I thought this quite strange and not indicative of a good recovery. In the meantime, the patients became weaker; purple spots appeared in their skin. Then they died a few days later.

The second process was as follows. After I had spread zinc oxide oil on the burns, they would within twenty-four hours begin to exude a pasty effusion which rapidly turned purulent. As the oil, itself of a pasty texture and colour, completely covered the festering surface of the burns, the ensuing purulence spread rapidly and widely. Indeed, it wasn't possible to tell zinc oxide oil from pus. But, day after day, I went on applying the oil to the patients' burns while they cried out in their agony and because of the heat. Flies swarmed on their suppurating wounds, which gave off a bad smell. I was unaware that this effusion of pus continually and reciprocally helped germs multiply on account of the decrease in the white corpuscle count in the patients' bloodstreams.

It became part of the routine for Mr Kawano and myself to visit our respective patients outside the hospital during the afternoons. I called on Mr Yamada, Mr Mizoguchi, Mr Kinoshita, Mr Yamagami, and their families. I treated the wound in Mr Yamada's leg and the lacerated wound in the head of Mr Mizoguchi. By now, most of them had left the air-raid shelters and were lying in the shelter of planks jutting out from or leaning against a hillside bank. Mr Yamada was improving slightly, but Mr Mizoguchi's head-wound was beginning to dry out. It wasn't a very good symptom. These patients were also rather weak and listless.

Miss Kinoshita's back was still embedded with a large number – maybe more than a hundred – of glass fragments, like a design in mother-of-pearl. Those many pieces of glass more deeply buried in the muscles had still to be extracted, even though I had been treating her injuries for three days. The glass-cuts had dried up in an abnormal way, with little bleeding of the scar tissue. She had become so weak she could only speak in a whisper. Soon she was dead. As for the Yamagamis, Mr Yamagami was glad that his four surviving children seemed to be getting better. But his wife had now been taken to the hospital, her burns were so severe. He continued to look after his wife in the hospital and his children in the burnt-out ruins of his house. Those four children were destined to be robbed of their lives later but neither their father nor I knew it as yet.

Returning to the hospital late one afternoon, I found a naval surgeon, a lieutenant, helped by four men from the medical corps, attending to the patients. He paid no attention to me, even though I was the resident doctor. What impertinence, I said to myself indignantly.

It was no use my getting angry, however. I probably looked nothing like a doctor; my dark-blue business suit was stained with blood, dirt and mercurochrome – I had been wearing it since before 9 August. I had straw sandals on my feet; I had grown quite thin and hadn't shaved for days. His failure to take me for a doctor was understandable. The hospital looked nothing like a first-aid hospital either. He must have thought that each of the injured, having lost their homes, had come here without leave, spread straw on the blackened floors of the fire-burnt ruin and then laid themselves down.

The naval officer and his four assistants went on tending the sick and injured in total disregard of me and the nurses. Holding long pincettes in both hands, they soaked large strips of gauze in a yellow oil called Rivanol, and laid them on burns and wounds. I watched their speedy and skilful treatment of the patients in admiration. Probably they had treated countless numbers of such wretched and badly burnt people at the military hospital in Omura or at Kawatana. My patients had only been treated by the application of mercurochrome and zinc oxide oil. It probably seemed to them that these pieces of gauze soaked in Rivanol were the newest, the greatest miracle in medicine.

After having treated about thirty patients in three hours, they stopped work and prepared to leave, saying: 'We've run out of supplies.'

I said to their leader in some confusion: 'To tell the truth, I'm the doctor in charge of this hospital. It was very kind of you to come here. Have you done all you can?'

The lieutenant, who looked quite young and boyish, said, 'We've got to go – we haven't any more supplies.'

'But you'll come again tomorrow? You'll treat them again tomorrow, won't you?'

I wanted him to promise me he would.

'I don't know,' he said. 'Tomorrow is another day.'

He was impersonal – and unwilling to commit himself.

I felt helpless: the patients would lose hope if they were unable to receive any more of such treatment. They would only become even more miserable. Again I begged him to return the next day and to treat the wretched people in my care, or else provide us with a military truck to take them to some better-equipped hospital, or at least supply me with some medicines. He turned away, saying he would do what he could, though he could promise nothing.

I thought: They were only a day-relief squad after all. I envied this doctor who could simply leave the moment his medical supplies ran out. I couldn't escape from these 130 sick, injured and tubercular patients; they were like a chain around my legs, or a heavy burden on my back.

I watched him go, biting my lip and with my eyes full of tears. How I wished I could run away and hide!

The next day the naval lieutenant paid another unexpected visit to the hospital. He brought a small amount of Rivanol, some potassium permanganate and several long pincettes. As a doctor, he must have understood how inadequate I felt, though he didn't express this either by word or look.

He said: 'I think, since this is a first-aid station, you ought to try to improve things here, however slightly, rather than send anyone to another hospital. I'm very short of supplies and equipment myself. But I'll share what I have with you, although I know it isn't enough.'

So saying, he gave me what he had brought: the finest gifts he could offer. I thanked him from the bottom of my heart for his generosity and promised I would try to improve conditions at the hospital. He went away. He had worn the uniform of a naval lieutenant even though, as it turned out, the Japanese navy was already defeated. That meant nothing to me then – I only wished the young lieutenant could have helped a little more.

At night, the droning of enemy planes overhead seemed to

become more insistent. But we were, by now, quite weak and apathetic. Our will-power and physical strength were fast deteriorating. More and more people were dying in the city below.

Father Ishikawa had been taken to Hongawachi, so Father Tagami of the Mary Society went about the noisome wards, offering up prayers for the dead and the seriously injured. Several were on the verge of death. I was present one night when one of the badly burnt victims breathed his last in a pitch-black room, lit by a single candle. I looked on with my arms folded, saying not a word. Father Tagami gave the man his last rites. Outside, Motohara lay silent in the night. Nothing but the father's prayers could be heard. 'May the soul of this man now rest in peace, through the grace of God.' I was not a Christian, but the more pain that was suffered by the body, the more I wished for the soul to rest in eternal peace.

In Tokyo, the projected military coup was set for 10 a.m. on 14 August, arrangements now having been made to deal with the Japanese leaders, civil and military, who might stand in the rebels' way. General Anami, much needed by the disaffected officers as their figurehead, would not commit himself, although he expressed his doubts about the coup's *success. Meanwhile, a 'peace warning' had gone to all American combatants in the Pacific: no military actions or attacks were to be made for the next twelve hours.*

At 8 a.m. on 14 August, General Anami asked his Chief of Staff, General Umezu, whether he would support a coup. 'Absolutely not!' said Umezu. 'The people won't follow you. Forty per cent of the factory workers have left their jobs already. We could never carry on the war under these conditions.' About the same time, Marquis Kido, the Lord Privy Seal and one of the Emperor's closest advisors, was given one of the leaflets that American planes were dropping all over Japan advocating surrender. He realized that they could have the opposite effect on certain elements of the population, and especially on the army. He saw the Emperor at about 9 a.m., as did Premier Suzuki, and the War Cabinet plus government heads were summoned to a meeting in the Imperial Palace at 10.30 a.m. All concerned abandoned their machinations and manoeuvring and rushed to obey, hastily donning the formal and proper attire for such a meeting. It took place in the underground conference room below the library. The War Cabinet and other ministers of state sat facing a narrow table covered with gold brocade, and beyond it a straight-backed, wooden chair. They rose and bowed as the Emperor entered, in full military dress and wearing white gloves. They all sat. Once more the opposing factions argued the rights and wrongs of the situation. Then the Emperor spoke. Pausing often to control himself and his voice, he said he considered the American reply was acceptable. Tears ran down his cheeks. He tried to explain his fears and feelings about the future, about handing his forces, his people and his country into the hands of the enemy. He said: 'As the Emperor Meiji once endured the unendurable, so shall I and so must you. If there is anything more that should be done I will do it . . . It is my desire that you, my ministers of state, accede to my wishes and forthwith accept the Allied reply.'

His ministers, his generals, his admirals, wept openly. The war was over: Japan had been defeated for the first time in her history. She had lost her honour and the war.

Without the Emperor's personal decision to end the war, against the advice of his army and navy Chiefs of Staff, it would have continued, and the Americans would have been forced to manufacture and use more atomic bombs and to undertake the invasion of Kyushu, codenamed Olympic, planned for 1 November 1945. Without the Emperor's personal intervention, the conquest of Japan would have been the bloodiest in history, and the Japanese armies overseas would have fought on until all were wiped out.

At 11.25 p.m. on 14 August, Emperor Hirohito recorded a radio broadcast to his people; it would be transmitted the following day at noon. Soon after midnight, a group of young officers, led by Major Hatanaka, staged a disorganized coup. *General Mori, who commanded the Imperial Guards at the Palace, was killed. But officers at the Eastern Army HQ in Tokyo refused to join the rebels. There was confusion and gunfire in the Palace and in the streets as rebel soldiers sought out those they thought had betrayed Japan; their houses were set on fire. At 4.30 a.m. General Anami, after drinking wine with friends, went into a corridor in his bungalow; he knelt and slashed his stomach with a knife. Then he stuck the knife in his neck. It took him three hours to die. Meanwhile, a desperate search by rebel officers failed to find the recording the Emperor had made, and at 4.35 a.m. Major*

Hatanaka rushed to the studios of NHK and at gun-point ordered the announcer to let him speak to the nation on the 5 a.m. news. An air-raid alert happened to be in progress, and the announcer told Hatanaka that he would have to get permission from the Eastern Army HQ, who took control of broadcasting during alerts. Hatanaka argued; then the telephone rang – it was the Eastern Army HQ. Permission to make the broadcast was refused, and General Tanaka, commander of the Eastern Army, went to the Palace to break up the rebellion; it petered out at dawn.

Hatanaka and two other leading rebels committed suicide in the park outside the Palace. Tokyo awoke to a new day, unaware of what had happened in the night.

In America, thirteen hours behind in time, it was still the night before. In the Oval Room at the White House, President Truman told his assembled heads of state and war that a note had been received – Japan had unconditionally surrendered. All night America celebrated, wild with joy.

On Wednesday, 15 August, I was awakened by someone singing: it came from above me. It appeared that mass was being celebrated somewhere in the ruined hospital. A fair number of people had gathered in the dining room on the first floor. Today was the day commemorating the Ascension of the Virgin Mary. Disregarding the mass, I set about seeing the patients after breakfast. It looked as if it was going to be another hot day.

The instances of bloody excrement, dysentery and purpura were on the increase. I couldn't think why. Even if a patient didn't die, his gums bled and his hair fell out. Burns and contusions suppurated at an alarming rate, extensively and out of control. I was totally at a loss to know how to deal with it all.

When Mr Kawano came back from the town that morning he said: 'The bomb seems to have been an atomic bomb. I read about it in a leaflet.' The leaflets had apparently been scattered by American planes.

'So it's true – an atomic bomb! Atomic energy!' I exclaimed.

About eleven o'clock Miss Fukahori, who had gone back to live in No. 3 district of Motohara town, came to the ruined entrance porch of the hospital with some out-patients and said: 'I think it's time at last for Japan to accept unconditional

97

surrender.' I wasn't very surprised at her words. I felt she could well be right. She added: 'It's said that at noon His Majesty the Emperor will make a very important announcement on the radio.'

The important announcement probably meant surrender. It was hardly likely to be a call for all-out resistance. I found it difficult to imagine that His Majesty the Emperor would appeal to all of us to die rather than surrender while so many innocent people were suffering so much. But, arising from a secret belief in the invincible might of Japan, another rumour had it that hundreds of aeroplanes were hidden away somewhere, and I was afraid that some rash and fatal counter-attack might yet be mounted.

Just then two policemen happened to pass by. They said to the chief nurse: 'Where did you hear that? It's nothing but a rumour, and absolute lies.' They took her away to the police station, saying: 'We have some questions to ask you. Come along with us.'

They were full of bluff, denying any possibility of unconditional surrender. Nonetheless, I was half in doubt about it myself – although I hoped the war would not continue a minute longer.

At about noon an enemy plane flew over the city, circling at quite a low altitude – so low, in fact, that one felt one could almost touch it. We hid in the basement. I saw what appeared to be British insignia on the plane's wings. It kept circling but gave no sign of dropping any bombs.

I said: 'It's strange that an enemy plane should do nothing but fly low over us, and a British one at that. We haven't seen any British planes before.'

As we learned later, it was about this time that the Japanese government surrendered unconditionally to the United States, Britain and the other Allied Powers. The low-altitude flight proved to have been a triumphal circuit of Nagasaki. Not knowing this, the sick and injured, the nurses and I, had all run about to escape from anticipated bursts of machine-gun fire.

As it happened, I never listened to His Majesty the Emperor speaking on the radio at noon. To begin with, there wasn't any radio set, and in any case, I was busy going the rounds of my patients, trying to deal with purulent wounds, burns, lacerations and the incomprehensible bleeding disease.

As dusk fell, Mr Kawano came back from Isahaya, bearing some new medical supplies.

'I listened to His Majesty on the radio in Isahaya,' he said. 'Japan has agreed to unconditional surrender.'

So at last the war was truly over. We had some idea of what unconditional surrender meant, but I wasn't concerned with how bitter the terms of surrender might turn out to be. I simply felt relieved to hear that the war had ended.

'What will become of Japan after this unconditional surrender?' asked one of the patients.

I said: 'I would rather surrender than suffer any more from these new bombs.'

Mr Kawano, who was a Protestant, was pleased that the war was over. I didn't myself feel particularly sad about the surrender. He went out again somewhere, and when he came back late at night he said: 'I hear that some army leaders tried to interrupt the broadcast and that they still advocate all-out resistance. General Anami, the Army minister, has killed himself.'

During the last few days I had thought only of the wounded, the dead and the in-patients. But suddenly Japan's situation and that of the world set my mind in a whirl. A picture of the wise and dignified face of General Anami presented itself to me. The scene of his suicide by disembowelment, *harakiri*, like an old-time Samurai, could all too easily be imagined.

'How foolish,' I said. 'What's the use of taking responsibility for the defeat when it's all over?'

I sat down in the yard. Around me sat Mr Kawano, Brother Iwanaga and Mr Noguchi, as well as Miss Murai and some of the in-patients with mild cases of TB or light injuries. Someone was weeping in the dark. I was also moved to tears, but by the thought of a surrender that had come too late for so many, not by the surrender itself.

An old poem, a fine piece of verse, says: 'A nation may be destroyed, yet its mountains and rivers will remain. Spring shall come to the ruins of the castle as before, and the grass and the leaves of the trees will be thick and green again.'

But there was now nothing poetic in my mood. Japan had been defeated, and nothing but ruin was left behind, with tens of thousands of people butchered, roasted, broken and in pain.

*

The next day I walked down into the city to view the new Japan.

An area of about five kilometres, from Ueno town to Nagasaki Station, was littered with a mass, an unending carpet of what looked like pebbles. As far as the eye could see there were nothing but pebbles, a peculiar desert of broken bits of stone, fragments of shattered roof-tiles, each three or four centimetres long. In Matsuyama town, above which the atomic bomb had exploded, the naturally dark-grey colour of the tiles had become red or orange-yellow, and they were pitted with pores as in pumice stone. The further away one went from Matsuyama town, the larger the broken tiles became as their colour turned black, so illustrating the variations in strength, heat and pressure of the blast. Iwakawa town, Hamaguchi town, Matsuyama town and Ohashi town had been entirely destroyed; nothing recognizable remained. I could barely distinguish the roads.

Electricity poles stood aslant, like bent and half-burnt bits of firewood or used matches. Those in Matsuyama had been burnt to the core and looked like sticks of charcoal. As one went further from Matsuyama town, the degree of carbonization became less, as well as the angles of inclination. It was strange to see them listing to one side or the other.

There had been a street-car service between Nagasaki Station and Ohashi town. Street-cars now stood on the tracks at regular intervals; some with their body-work crushed, leaning one way. A car in the Matsuyama area had been reduced to a skeleton; it must have burst into flames in an instant – all that was left was its bent iron frame. Its passengers had been carbonized like the electricity poles.

The iron frameworks of the Mitsubishi Ordnance Factory and the Mitsubishi Steel Works were twisted and bowed like pieces of wire. Yamazato Primary School, Shiroyama Primary School, Chinzei Gakuin Secondary School and the three-storeyed ferro-concrete building of Nagasaki Hospital had been crushed by blast pressure and their interiors ravaged by fire. Their windows had been blown out, leaving gaping, dark and ominous holes in the walls.

We would never again see the red Romanesque domes of Urakami Church, which had once claimed to be the most splendid place of Christian worship in the East. Now an ungainly pile of bricks, it looked like a huge comb with broken and missing teeth. Very close to the epicentre, situated on a small hill, had stood the city jail, surrounded by a slanting concrete wall. Several hundred prisoners had been burnt to death in an instant within its walls.

The charred and splintered sticks like broom-handles that stuck up here and there had once been trees. Even the surrounding and formerly green hills were scorched brown or covered in ashes.

The sun shone down upon the ruined town. It made me sad to see the apparatus of civilization – the tilting and fallen electricity poles, the telegraph wires hanging low, the water-pipes broken and spouting water – in the midst of all the wreckage. The water, bubbling out without a care, put me in mind of the people who once had lived there. No smoke issued from any chimney; and some were crooked, leaning away from the blast.

A highway used to run from Nagasaki Station to Sumiyoshi, Michinoo and Togitsu. It was just identifiable. The only people to be seen were moving along it, creeping from Nagasaki Station to Michinoo and back again. Some, as they walked, looked only at the road, as if searching for something they had lost.

The defeat and surrender of Japan, the end of the war, caused no excitement in Urakami and Nagasaki, which had been in ruins since 9 August. There was hardly anyone there to get excited, and nothing to be excited about: there was no object which had not been scorched or destroyed, no person who had escaped injury or death. We now heard more about the important broadcast made by the Emperor the day before. Some military leaders had almost prevented it being broadcast, and it was said that the army's First Division, with the Emperor as their unwilling leader, had plotted to fight it out to the end. Apparently, a militant group in the army had insisted on fighting to the last man, urging all-out national resistance against America and Britain for the sake of maintaining Japan's national identity and pride. But such rumours and alarms faded away in a day or two like an ebbing tide.

I was continually asked by the in-patients and the staff: 'What will become of Japan, of our hospital and us?'

I couldn't see far into the future of Japan, nor was I sure of our personal future. All I could say was: 'The Americans and British aren't monsters, but human beings like us. This war has been different from any other, but they won't harm you any more, or cause you any more pain. Things will never be as bad as this again.'

When Mr Kawano returned from the city, bringing an extra edition of the *Domei Press* with him, it was getting on towards evening. It was now Thursday, 16 August, a week after the bomb had fallen. In the gathering dusk I was eating rice-balls out in the yard with Brother Iwanaga, Mr Noguchi, the nurses and the in-patients. The news extra, printed on a small sheet of coarse paper, contained yesterday's broadcast by His Majesty the Emperor.

Taking it from Mr Kawano in silence, I read it over. As I read on, some inspiration surged through me like an incoming tide. I got to my feet and called out in the darkening yard: 'Your attention please! I would like you to listen to this.'

Those patients who were able to walk came up and gathered around me. Someone standing behind held a candle so that its light fell onto the paper, onto the Emperor's statement about the present desperate plight of Japan.

At first I read aloud, but gradually my voice faded away: 'To our good and loyal subjects. After pondering deeply the general trends of the world, and the actual conditions obtaining in our Empire today, we have decided to effect a settlement of the present situation by resorting to an extraordinary measure. We have ordered our government to communicate to the governments of the United States, Great Britain, China and the Soviet Union that our Empire accepts the provisions of their Joint Declaration . . . The war has lasted nearly four years. Despite the best that has been done by everyone – the gallant fighting of military and naval forces, the diligence and assiduity of our servants of the State, and the devoted service of our one hundred million people – the war situation has developed not necessarily to Japan's advantage, while the general trends of the world have all turned against her interest. Moreover, the enemy has begun to employ a new and most cruel bomb, the power of which to do damage is indeed incalculable, taking the toll of many innocent lives. Should we continue to fight, it would not only result in an ultimate collapse and obliteration of the Japanese nation, but

would also lead to the total extinction of human civilization . . .
The thought of those officers and men, as well as others who
have fallen in the field of battle, those who have died at their
posts of duty, or those who have met with untimely death, and
all their bereaved families, pains our heart night and day. The
welfare of the wounded and the war-sufferers, and of those who
have lost their homes and livelihood, are the objects of our
profound solicitude.'

It was all too late. As I read on, I wanted to ask why our
leaders had found it necessary to call down such misery on us in
the furtherance of what they had called a sacred war?

I read on softly: 'We are keenly aware of all of you, our
subjects . . . However, we have resolved to pave the way for a
grand peace for all the generations to come by enduring the
unendurable and suffering what is unsufferable . . . Unite your
total strength to be devoted to the construction of the future.
Cultivate the ways of rectitude, foster nobility of spirit; and
work with resolution so you may enhance the innate glory of the
Imperial State and keep pace with the progress of the world.'

I read through the statement with frequent pauses. Most of
the others were weeping silently, the nurses were sobbing aloud.
At the end I murmured dejectedly: 'You lost your families and
your homes when the atomic bomb exploded – now you have
lost your country.'

But, at the same time, this realization that we had lost
everything seemed to take a load off my mind. For now we had
nothing left to lose.

*Throughout Japan people wept on hearing the news, although the
Emperor's broadcast, spoken in the lilting, elaborate language of
the court, was understood by few. But at noon all traffic had
stopped in the cities as people stood and bowed their heads to hear
him. The government resigned; an uncle of Hirohito's was
appointed in place of Premier Suzuki. At Oita airfield, late in the
afternoon, eleven naval fighter-bombers, led by Admiral Ugaki,
took off on a final kamikaze mission, heading for Okinawa. They
were never heard of again. At dusk, in Tokyo, General Anami's
uniformed body was cremated on Ichigaya hill.*

That afternoon a message was sent to the Emperor and his

government saying that the sender had been designated as the Supreme Commander for the Allied Powers and had been empowered to arrange the cessation of hostilities at the earliest practicable date.

The main message dealt with details concerning the future use of radio communications. It was signed 'MacArthur'.

4

As soon as the war came to an end, the words 'atomic bomb' began to be passed from mouth to mouth and to fill the people in the hospital with apprehension and fear.

On about 13 August, the surviving professors at Nagasaki Medical College had got hold of some leaflets on which the royal crest of the chrysanthemum was emblazoned. These were leaflets which had been scattered from the sky by American planes. They said:

> People of Japan! The terrible weapon that destroyed Hiro-shima and Nagasaki was an atomic bomb. For your own sake you should ask His Majesty the Emperor to bring this war to an end and surrender as soon as possible.

Nagasaki Medical College, that sanctuary of medical science, had been built of wood and had stood not far from the epicentre of the explosion, and so its destruction was disastrous beyond description. The professors and assistant professors in each department had for the most part perished wherever they happened to be in the laboratories or in the lecture theatre; a very few managed to escape with their lives.

The college hospital, although it was built of ferro-concrete and stood a little further away from the epicentre, was also completely destroyed. In the building at the time there were not only several professors and assistant professors, but also a number of doctors and nurses, and hundreds of patients. In an instant, they were consigned to a hell full of agonized cries, black smoke and crimson flame.

That night, those of them who were dying and those who were lucky enough to have escaped from the hospital without apparent injury, lay down in air-raid shelters at the rear of the hospital buildings, at the foot of the hill of Kompira. Although they had several skilful doctors among them and lay close to the centre of Nagasaki's main seat of medical knowledge, they died one after the other, despite anything that could be done for them. Many had blood-stained diarrhoea and developed symptoms of dysentery. Some, carried to the Mangyoji Temple in Togitsu town, died in quick succession within a couple of days.

President Tsunoo, who was giving a lecture when the bomb exploded, was injured in the head and back by pieces of flying glass. On the following day, he began to cough up some blood and his excrement became bloody. He made a diagnosis of his own condition and concluded that the symptoms were those of dysentery. He said he would treat himself accordingly, believing that the army hospital would have an appropriate and adequate supply of medicine.

Fortunately, his colleague Professor Koyano had not been seriously injured, and was able to travel to the army hospital and obtain appropriate drugs. This hospital was situated in Hago-rama town, far enough from the epicentre to have escaped damage, and the director, a lieutenant-colonel, had once been among Professor Koyano's students. He was able to get a new medicine for dysentery, which was regarded as very valuable in those days. But it had no effect on Dr Tsunoo. Haemorrhage and nausea were, in his case, not symptoms of dysentery, but rather those of radiation sickness.

After 14 August, after the professors had read those leaflets revealing the dreadful nature of the bomb, they realized that they were confronted not with dysentery but with an unknown and terrible atomic disease, and none of them knew how to deal with it. The colossal heat produced by the bomb and the gigantic blast effect *were* capable of comprehension, once it was known that they were produced by atomic energy. But from now on all doctors and medical men in Nagasaki were faced with trying to understand and treat diseases and illness caused by radiation. The professors at the medical college wrestled with the effects and cure of radiation sickness from then on, day and night, risking their own lives and, so to speak, using themselves as guinea-pigs. So did we in Urakami Hospital, and lived in fear for forty days, faced with a new enemy that we could not even see.

Another kind of leaflet was found which had also been thrown from the sky by the US Air Force. It read as follows:

We advise the Japanese people to read this leaflet carefully. The United States now possesses the most powerful explosive that has ever been invented. A single atomic bomb has as great an explosive power as all the bombs that would be carried by two thousand B29s. You should carefully consider this fearful fact, and we assure you, in the name of God, that it is absolutely true. We have now begun to use this weapon against Japan. If you still have any doubts about its destructive capabilities, consider what happened when only one atomic bomb was dropped on Hiroshima. We advise you to beg His Majesty the Emperor to bring the war to an end, before we use this bomb to destroy every military installation that is prolonging this senseless war. We advise you to take the necessary steps to establish a new, peace-loving Japan by accepting the thirteen items relating to an honourable surrender, of which the President of the United States has recently given you an outline. You should at once take all the necessary steps to end all armed resistance – or we shall be forced to bring an immediate end to this war by unhesitatingly using this bomb as well as every other powerful weapon we have.

So at last it became clear to the Japanese people that the bombs dropped on Hiroshima and Nagasaki had been atomic ones. Even as the people of Japan extinguished fires with water from buckets, sharpened bamboo spears to act as weapons of self-defence and hunted for sweet potatoes to stave off hunger, so the Americans were making the atomic bomb. And, having made it, they dropped one bomb on Hiroshima on 6 August and another on Nagasaki on 9 August.

Scientists in America and Britain knew a great deal about the atomic bomb, about its power and energy – but they knew far less about the actual effects of radioactivity on human beings. The effects of radiation upon living creatures could be studied by exposing animals to them, mice, monkeys, guinea-pigs or dogs, upon all of which American scientists must have made many experiments. But such experiments had never been made on human beings.

Rumours flew about. It was said that for seventy-five years no creature could live in areas devastated by an atomic bomb. It was said that for seventy-five years no human life could exist in Nagasaki or Hiroshima.

These rumours turned out to be based upon results obtained from the A-bomb test in Nevada. Nonetheless, the people of Nagasaki and Hiroshima had continued to search for survivors in the ruins, nursing them not far from the epicentre, and continuing to live in the devastated city where it was thought no creature could survive during the next three quarters of a century.

A second cousin of mine, a Fleet Air Arm commander in Sasebo, arrived in the ruins of Urakami Hospital on 20 August.

He said: 'Dr Akizuki, why don't you leave this place and come with me to Oita? If you remain here, you'll probably die.'

Oita was my parents' home town, where two of my married sisters also lived. Anxious about my safety, he advised me to leave Nagasaki.

I replied: 'No, I'll stay. Anyway, it's too late now – my life or death has already been determined. It doesn't matter.'

When it came to it I was unable to abandon the people in my care. I was not alone in my resolve. Other doctors, in Hiroshima and Nagasaki, had the courage to confront the fatal diseases caused by radiation on the very ground where the ashes of radioactive substances lay, even though they also had been injured in the explosion and exposed to its deadly rays. They fought their battles without instruments or adequate nursing. It was not a question of medical art or science – it was a basic struggle against death, a cry for life.

I myself became aware of the symptoms of radiation sickness from about 13 August, even though I remained in ignorance as to their cause. The symptoms first appeared in those victims who had been injured near Urakami Church. The mother of the chief nurse, injured at Motoo town, had been similarly affected before she died in the hospital. After 16 August such cases increased rapidly in number. So far I had done what I could for people whose bodies had been burnt or those who had been wounded by glass or injured by falling beams. Now the symptoms of the unknown disease, which I had previously thought to be dysentery or purpura, became quite general: feelings of nausea, feelings of lethargy, loss of hair, bloody excrement, mulberry spots on the skin, the gums beginning to bleed. The symptoms suddenly appeared in certain patients who had no apparent injuries. They intensified within a day or two, after which the patients died. In other cases, the symptoms emerged gradually over the period of a week. Their development also resulted in the patients' death. In some patients, where the symptoms were far less acute, the patients did escape death, but the symptoms varied from person to person. The virulence or otherwise of the disease seemed to depend on the patients' powers of resistance and also upon their age. All I could be sure of was this: that the degree of radiation sickness depended upon the victim's distance from the epicentre. I was not quite sure where the epicentre was, but those patients from Motoo town, Hashiguchi town, Urakami Church and Ueno town seemed to be the most seriously affected. The sisters from Josei Girls' School were similarly smitten, and those victims who came from the No. 1 district of Motohara came next in the severity of their symptoms. Yet a strong young man like Mr Kawano, who had escaped uninjured from the medical college, miraculously survived.

Besides trying to cope with all the problems of those who had been burnt and injured, I now had to work out some way of dealing with and searching for a remedy for the effects of radiation sickness.

After about 15 August, the chief nurse, Brother Iwanaga, Miss Murai and I became increasingly tired. At first I thought that sleeping in the open air for nearly a week had exhausted me, causing a fatigue which made me feel as if I had been beaten all over my body. Until then I connected nothing of this with any atomic disease or radiation sickness. But now I began to consider my weariness and other symptoms objectively.

At one time I had worked for a year as an assistant to Professor Nagai, the departmental head of radiotherapeutics at Nagasaki College Hospital. While working in radiotherapy I came across the symptom known as 'Röntgen catarrh'. This occurred when X-rays probed deeply into conditions of uterine cancer or mammary cancer. The continued use of X-rays caused the patient to feel ill several days later. We called the condition 'Röntgen catarrh'. At that time our college hospital was so short of doctors that I had many patients to examine – and, in the process, I tired myself out. I was X-raying the insides of two or three patients a day, continuing to do this from Monday to Friday. On Saturday I stopped and analysed the results or held a discussion meeting. I have never had a very strong constitution, and one Friday I began to feel ill. When I told a senior colleague, he informed me that what I had must be Röntgen catarrh.

On about 15 August 1945 it became clear to me that my present symptoms were exactly like those caused by Röntgen catarrh.

X-rays are, in terms of classical physics, electromagnetic waves with ultra-short wavelengths which pass through the cells of the human body and can destroy them. The kind of cell which was destroyed by the Röntgen rays was that in the tissue, where frequent fissions took place. Something like this was happening after the A-bomb explosion. But I still had no idea of the kind of rays the A-bomb had produced. I made a diagnosis and reasoned thus: they could be radium rays, Röntgen rays, gamma rays, or something similar, which probably destroyed any haematogenic tissue, the marrow tissue of the human body. As a result, many patients at the hospital were showing symptoms of something like purpura.

I had neither a corpuscle-calculating machine nor enough apparatus, or, indeed, the strength, to dye corpuscles and examine them under a microscope – nothing but my own imagination and powers of deduction. I tried to remember how we had treated Röntgen catarrh. Once, in the department of radiotherapy, when the patients and I were afflicted with catarrh, I drank and also made them drink a solution of salt which contained more salt than a physiological salt solution – and this had proved effective. Indeed, at that time a saline solution to

110

combat catarrh was generally agreed by doctors to be the best remedy.

Now I went about saying: 'Salt is good for victims of the bomb. I assure you, salt can be most useful in effecting a cure. Take as much as you can.'

I had no knowledge of the new biophysics or of atombiology – no books, no treatises about atomic disease. Yet I became convinced of the validity of my method of dietetics – mineral dietetics – which could simply be defined as follows: salt or a natrium ion gave vitality to the haematogenic cells, while sugar was their toxin.

I felt something like confidence welling up in my chest. I gave the cooks and the staff strict orders that, when they made the unpolished rice balls, they must add some salt to them, and make salty, thick miso soup at every meal, and never use any sugar. When they failed to follow my instructions, I scolded them remorselessly, saying: 'Don't ever take any sugar, nothing sweet!'

As it was, the in-patients and the staff had already been forbidden to use any sugar before the atomic bomb was dropped since sugar was generally in very short supply.

'What's so bad about sugar?' everyone asked. 'Why is salt so effective in the cure of atomic disease?'

I felt disinclined to explain the reasons in detail. I said: 'Sugar is bad for you – you have my word for it. Sugar will destroy your blood.'

This mineral method of curing atomic sickness which had flashed into my mind was put into practice by myself and by those who accepted my view.

Several other methods of curing atomic disease were tried and introduced: Professor Nagai's method, using vitamin B1 and glucose; Professor Kageura's method, using strong doses of vitamin C, that is, the sap decocted from persimmon leaves; or a method involving the consumption of Japanese *sake* or alcohol. But my mineral method, I still believe, made it possible for me to remain alive and to go on working as a doctor in Urakami Hospital – despite the fact that I did not possess a very strong constitution and had, moreover, suffered from the effects of the atomic bomb at a distance of about 1,600 metres. The radiation at that distance may not have been fatal, but, since the explosion, Brother Iwanaga, Mr Noguchi, the chief nurse, Miss Murai and I – as well as the rest of the staff and the in-patients – had gone on living in the contaminated ashes of the ruined city. I believe it was thanks to this salt cure – or Akizuki's dietetics – that each of us was able to work among the people and to care for them day after day, overcoming our fatigue and the symptoms of atomic disease and eventually to survive the disaster. I and those around me believed this then, even though the academics were dubious about this, and still are.

When August was twenty days old, the nights began to grow more chilly little by little, although it was still scorching hot by day. Night-dews began to fall, so we could no longer sleep out of doors under the stars. I slept in the patients' bathroom in the basement, and Brother Iwanaga slept in the kitchen. More mosquitoes appeared; striped mosquitoes, of which we had seen no signs for a while, arrived again in large numbers.

When night came, fires blazed brightly down in the town below as they had done, night after night, for ten successive days. They were still cremating corpses. The glow of these little fires could be seen from far away. I reflected on how, when the Black Death raged through the large cities and towns of Europe long ago, the victims had likewise been burnt, as well as their houses. And I also reflected on how, during the rebellion of 1467 to 1477 in the reign of the Emperor Oonin, the city of Kyoto had been repeatedly set on fire during a series of battles until at last all that was left was a great waste of smoking ruins.

I said to Mr Noguchi: 'It's just the same now as it was then; mankind has made no progress. We always flatter ourselves that we have become wiser and more civilized. But the facts show we are as senseless and as savage as ever.'

He and I took it upon ourselves to deal with the corpses.

The half-naked body of one unidentified man lay in a corner of the hospital yard. It had already turned black and was swarming with flies. We could hardly leave it as it was. We made arrangements for it to be cremated in the east end of the yard. Three sheets of corrugated iron were piled up, one on top of the other, and on top of them we heaped some firewood, on which the body was laid. After dark it was cremated.

Brother Iwanaga, Mr Noguchi and I stood around the funeral

pyre. I set light to the kindling; the flames caught hold. Soon the body was burning, being consumed by somewhat darker flames than those that came from the wood. Both Brother Iwanaga and Mr Noguchi lamented as they watched the body burn.

This cremation was carried out in the dusk of evening. The chief nurse and Miss Murai kept away; the hospital was silent.

When some seriously injured person taken in by the hospital died, the body would usually be claimed and taken away by the family or relations, if their homes had been in the neighbourhood. Any unclaimed body, however, was simply left lying in the east of the yard to await cremation. We carried out many cremations; the morning after a cremation Brother Iwanaga buried the bones in the chapel yard. Most of those whose bodies we burnt had been drafted as workers at the Mitsubishi Ordnance Factory or were members of a volunteer corps. We didn't know their names or where they had come from. These people must have had parents, wives, children, brothers and sisters. Later on, in fact, people came to the hospital from a long way away searching for missing relatives who had fallen victim to the atomic bomb. But this did not happen for another two or three months.

At the time I had no desire to know who these people were as I watched their bodies burn in the yard, in a ceremony that was solemn, sad and poorly attended. For all I knew, I myself might similarly be burnt to ashes a few days later or within a week. Life or death was a matter of chance, of fate, and the dividing line between the man being cremated and the doctor cremating him was slight. In the light of the flames that lit the dusk, Brother Iwanaga and I must have looked like supernatural creatures.

Towards 21 August, Mr Hayashi, who had been a hospital in-patient suffering from intestinal tuberculosis, took a sudden turn for the worse. Before the atomic bomb was dropped he had been seriously ill, troubled with a cough and congestion of the lungs. He had been safely carried out of the wrecked hospital, and since that day had lain on a bed on what had been the gymnasium floor. His only external wound had been caused by the piece of glass which had pierced his neck. But it turned out to be much more serious than at first appeared. He also suffered greatly every day from the stifling summer heat and grew weaker and weaker. His mother had remained with him after leaving Omura three days after the explosion, anxious about his safety. She had been delighted to find her son alive, and thought it was a miracle.

Harassed by the heat in the gymnasium by day and tormented by mosquitoes by night, Mr Hayashi continually fretted and complained like a child. He was anxious to return to Omura, but it was beyond the bounds of possibility to take him as far as Omura among all the confusion that followed the end of the war.

'I want to go home!' he cried.

His mother said soothingly: 'Soon, when you are a little better.'

He said to me, much concerned about the wound in his neck: 'Doctor, I can feel the air escape, hissing, from my neck just here, and when I put a finger on it, it becomes much easier to breathe.'

I was afraid the wound in his throat might prove to be fatal. But his tuberculosis was also killing him. In my stethoscope, rhonchi could be heard in both sides of his lungs as well as at the front and rear. He also suffered from serious diarrhoea.

It was towards day-break on 22 August that he breathed his last. He was the first of my in-patients to die after the A-bomb explosion.

I said to the chief nurse and Miss Murai: 'It must have been very uncomfortable for him, lying on a thin mattress on the cold concrete floor.'

'No,' said his mother. 'My son was a lucky boy. If it hadn't been for you, he would have been burnt to ashes in the hospital fire. He was fortunate to have been looked after so well to the end.'

It seemed she was very grateful to the hospital staff for staying on and taking care of the patients, even though the hospital had been gutted and all its supplies and equipment destroyed. Again I felt I wanted to apologize, feeling personally responsible for the loss of all our painkillers and drugs.

Mr Hayashi's remains were properly laid out, and at dusk a cremation service was held in the hospital yard. He came of a Buddhist family. Watching the fiery smoke rise into the dusk, I murmured the Buddhist verse, 'Kimyo Muryoju Nyorai', which means 'I have infinite faith in Buddha.' It has the same meaning as 'Our Father which art in Heaven.' Brother Iwanaga said: 'May

114

the souls of the dead rest in peace through the mercy of Jesus Christ.' It was everyone's wish.

The next morning – it was two weeks now since the A-bomb explosion – I sent Mr Hayashi's mother back to Omura with his bones and a death certificate written on a scrap of paper which happened to be to hand. Hugging the bag containing her son's bones, she bowed over and over again before the nurses and those TB patients who still remained, expressing her gratitude and thanks.

On Friday, 24 August, news of the death of Dr Tsunoo, President of the Medical College Hospital, was brought to us by Mr Kawano, who had been a student there; he was naturally very upset. His death made Mr Kawano feel that Nagasaki Medical College, already physically destroyed, had finally ceased to exist.

At the news of Dr Tsunoo's death, the staff broke down one after the other. I was examining some patients smitten with radiation sickness when I heard of his death; some of them began to weep, and his death was a great shock to me personally. Not even he, I thought, has been able to stay alive. The patients said: 'If even Dr Tsunoo couldn't live, there can be no hope for us.'

Two days before the atomic bomb was dropped on Nagasaki, Dr Tsunoo had been on his way back to the city from Tokyo. He happened to pass through Hiroshima twenty-four hours after the bomb exploded there, and was able to see for himself as he walked through the city all the misery and devastation that had been caused. As a result, when he reached Nagasaki, he had to decide whether or not lectures at the college should continue now that the Americans had manufactured some horrendous weapon and had actually begun to drop it on Japanese cities. It was decided at an urgent meeting of the hospital professors that no lectures should be given on or after 10 August. One day was to make all the difference.

At 11.02 on 9 August, the bomb exploded in the air above Matsuyama town, its epicentre 600 metres away from Nagasaki Medical College. The huge burst of energy that was produced, equivalent to that of a solar flare, crushed what we called the 'Medical Palace' and turned it into a mass of flames. At that

115

moment, Dr Tsunoo was giving a dissertation to some students at the bedside of a patient. He had silver hair, but his face was youthful and full of animation. He was always an object of respect and admiration for both the teachers and the students, who couldn't help remarking on his strength of body and intellect.

Dr Tsunoo, blood pouring from his silver head and down his face, was carried from the out-patients' clinic on Mr Tomokiyo's back and taken up the hill at the rear of the college. He had seen the destruction wrought by the new bomb on Hiroshima, and now was faced with a sea of fire over five kilometres square, belching black and yellow smoke. Below him the college was in flames. Many doctors and nurses and hundreds of medical students had worked and studied there. More than that, several hundred patients lay in the college hospital, attended in many cases by families and relations. In the midst of all the carnage and burning wreckage, people ran about, seeking safety and shelter. Doctors and nurses, desperately concerned about their charges, tried to save them, only to be overwhelmed themselves by fire and smoke.

In the evening, Dr Tsunoo returned to the college hospital, accompanied by the chief nurse and his team of physicians from the Internal Medicine Division. In the tunnel-like air-raid shelter at the rear of the operating theatre, two improvised beds were set up side by side. Dr Tsunoo lay down on one of the beds; Professor Takagi, an anatomist, occupied the other. In a recess near-by, Professor Yamano, chief of the Ophthalmological Department, lay in agony – as did a surgeon, Assistant Professor Ishizaki.

Professor Takagi, who had been in the wooden lecture theatre of the department of anatomy, had luckily escaped injury, as the shattered roof and ceiling were held up by iron supports. But at midnight he began to suffer much pain; he vomited often. Lying on the next bed, Dr Tsunoo tried to determine what was wrong with him. He murmured: 'I can't make it out. It may be peritonitis.'

Two days later, on 11 August, Professor Takagi died, having suffered greatly from a virulent attack of the atomic disease. But even so skilled a physician as Dr Tsunoo had not been able to diagnose the cause.

The day before, his own faeces had begun to be stained with blood. Although Professor Koyano had obtained a special medicine used in the cure of dysentery, it had no effect. Dr Tsunoo continued to bleed internally. On 13 August he was carried to the Nameshi Shrine on a hand-cart. His friends and colleagues determined to save him at any cost and did all they could for him. But on 23 August he died. As he breathed his last, he besought them to rebuild the college hospital one day.

When the atomic bomb exploded, Dr Tsunoo, in the out-patients' clinic, had been about 700 metres from the epicentre of the explosion. The clinic was built of reinforced concrete, and although he was injured, his injuries were apparently not fatal. But he remained in the vicinity of the hospital, surrounded by large quantities of radioactive substances. On top of this, he had walked for about five kilometres through the devastated city of Hiroshima on 7 August, traversing the carbonized desert created by the new bomb when he may also have been contaminated by radioactivity. A combination of these factors must have led to his death.

I was, as I have said, greatly disturbed when I heard that President Tsunoo had died – even he, who had received the finest medical care and the best available treatment, including vitamin B1, dextrose and heart stimulants. I felt as if the atomic disease were like some insidious and all-powerful evil spirit that plucked out our hair and sucked out our blood. I shuddered at the thought of such a fate befalling the injured, the TB patients and the staff in Urakami Hospital. On the other hand, it made me more determined than ever to continue with my own method of treatment, based on a diet of miso soup, unpolished rice and, above all, salt. Sugar, my dictum had it, was poison to the blood. Stubbornly I persuaded the people around me to do as I said, repeating my instructions over and over again. I became a man possessed.

The real terror caused by the atomic bomb lasted for a period of forty to fifty days, from the middle of August to the end of September. During this time, Brother Iwanaga, Mr Noguchi, the nurses, the in-patients, all those who dwelt on the hill of Motohara, and I existed from day to day, struggling for survival, confronted at every moment of each day with the fact and fear of dying and death. During this period, the confusion and breakdown of civilization created by the bomb was at its height, and food supplies, rescue work, medical treatment and information were woefully inadequate.

We were now able to label our unknown adversary 'atomic disease' or 'radioactive contamination' among other names. But they were only labels: we knew nothing about its cause or cure. We only knew that it had a fatal power that deprived us of our dearest friends, our wives and children. Those who happened to have been out of doors at a distance of 500, 1,000 or 1,500 metres from the epicentre when the A-bomb exploded were nearly all dead by the end of September. Some breathed their last in scorched fields of sweet potatoes, or among the burnt wild grass, while brother or sister, wife or child, looked after them; others died utterly alone.

Within seven to ten days after the A-bomb explosion, people began to die in swift succession. They died of the burns that covered their bodies and of acute atomic disease. Innumerable people who had been burnt turned a mulberry colour, like worms, and died. It was terrible, but death coming so suddenly, so abruptly, left me little time to brood. Even so, the ensuing forty days caused me much sorrow and grief. For the disease that infected the people – whether the atomic disease or some purulent condition associated with it – destroyed them little by little. As a doctor, I was forced to face the slow and certain deaths of my patients.

The Josei Girls' School in Ueno town, which had been founded by French nuns, was housed in an old, red-brick, two-storeyed building. When the Pacific War began, the European sisters at the convent were taken away and confined in a concentration camp in Kobe, including the elderly sisters who had devoted themselves for as many as sixty years to their Japanese pupils. Left on their own, the Japanese sisters struggled against many difficulties to keep the convent running.

With a shortage of nursing sisters in Urakami Hospital, Brother Iwanaga had pleaded for the assistance of two of the younger sisters who worked at the girls' school, Sister Tateishi and Sister Momota. They came to us for about six months, and worked very hard, caring for the tubercular patients alongside

Brother Iwanaga, the chief nurse, Miss Fukahori, Miss Murai and myself. However, in May 1945 they returned to Josei Girls' School to continue with their training and religious duties.

At 11.02 on 9 August 1945, the A-bomb exploded almost directly over the school and Urakami Church. The school was situated, in fact, about 500 or 600 metres from the epicentre, as we learnt later. Some months earlier, both the school and its kindergarten had been closed, and at the time of the explosion most of the pupils had already been conscripted as members of the volunteer corps working in the near-by ordnance factory. Accordingly, I never discovered exactly how many pupils remained at the school. Twenty-three sisters and novices were, however, in residence.

That morning, the pupils in the senior classes were out in the sun, labouring away with little picks and hatchets, digging up the roots of pine-trees in Akagi cemetery near the school, for turpentine oil could be extracted from the roots. At eleven o'clock the sun was already high above Kompira hill and it was scorching hot. The sisters of Josei Girls' School were also at work, instructing and showing the girl pupils what to do. Suddenly the atomic bomb exploded in an immense ball of fire above the Matsuyama district. Akagi cemetery was 200 or 300 metres away from the convent, but since it lay on high ground, the heat and the blast caused by the explosion were as great as if the sun itself had exploded and blasted them. The pine-trees were torn to shreds and pushed over, the tombstones of the Christians were overturned and hurled many yards, and, among them, the nuns and their pupils were thrown down and burnt. Some were killed on the spot; others, who had been badly burned, found their way home with great difficulty and pain; most of them died on their return. Two days later, on 11 August, the body of the principal was found under a fallen tombstone.

On 11 August, one of the nuns, Sister Mizoguchi, was carried on a stretcher to an air-raid shelter near her family home below the hospital, where her brother, Mr Mizoguchi, already lay, wounded in the head. Her shin-bone was visible through a terrible gash in her leg. Trapped for some time under a fallen tree, she was eventually pulled clear by some of the sisters. A rumour reached them that I was continuing to work as a doctor in Urakami Hospital. So they sent for me, and I visited the shelter in which Sister Mizoguchi lay. Already the symptoms of atomic disease were in evidence: the mucus membrane in her mouth as well as her skin had changed in colour and was now congested with purple spots. I did what I could for her, and for the other nuns who lay among the people in the shelter. But I knew there was nothing I could do to save them.

Stoically enduring her own pain, Sister Mizoguchi spoke words of comfort to me and those near her. Her features were those of the 'Maria' which used to hang in a corridor of our hospital. I knelt beside her. The wound in her leg seemed somehow like one of the wounds of Jesus. Why was it, I wondered, that such good and devout people had to be injured and killed?

'Doctor,' she whispered, 'you mustn't overtire yourself. You must look after yourself for the sake of everyone else.'

I said: 'You're just as important. More so. So you've got to get better, and soon, and I'm sure you will.'

'As God wills,' she said.

I was not a Catholic – I was a Buddhist. It was hard for me to understand the Catholic or Protestant Christian idea that everything could be attributed to the will and grace of God. It vexed me that these people believed pain and suffering were part of some divine plan. From bitter experience, I couldn't believe in such blind faith, and I mercilessly questioned Sister Mizoguchi and the other innocent, credulous nuns.

'Why is it that *you* have to suffer like this?' I demanded. 'Why people like you, who've done nothing but good? It isn't right!'

'I believe in providence,' they would reply feebly, but with a smile. 'It's the will of God.'

'How can God make you suffer so much after all your prayers and the selfless good you've done?' I asked.

I didn't mean to be cruel, questioning such severely burnt people like that. But I had often asked myself such questions; they had troubled my mind for days, ever since 9 August – no, ever since I became resident doctor at Urakami Hospital in September 1944.

Now the dreadful spectacle of the pain and misery of these pathetic sisters made me doubt yet again the providence of God. But they responded to all my savage questions with a smile, despite their agony.

'We have sinned,' they said. 'We are human, not divine.' Sister

120

Mizoguchi murmured: 'I'm sure, Dr Akizuki, like any good Catholic, you would wish to save the souls as well as the bodies of the sick and injured. For my sake, try to do so as you tend them. Let them rest in peace.'

I felt abashed, but at the same time most bitter about the A-bomb which had so grievously injured even those whose lives were devoted to prayer and the service of others. I cursed the Americans who had dropped the bomb, and more than ever hated the Japanese government who had wilfully perpetuated this senseless war. I blamed the one and then the other, but on no one could I actually vent my bitterness and censure.

The sisters in the air-raid shelter coughed up blood and, vilely discoloured, died four or five days later, the murmuring of their prayers echoing about them in the shelter. Sister Mizoguchi also died, before I had finished treating the gaping wound in her shin. Death seized the lives of all twenty-three sisters and each of them died from radiation sickness.

All the people who fell victim to the bomb and who had happened to be within 500 metres of the epicentre died before 15 August. After that, nearly all those people who had been within 500 and 1,500 metres of the explosion slowly died, one after the other, between then and the end of September. The difference in their time of dying depended on the quantity of radioactive rays they absorbed, on their physical condition and their exact location at the moment of explosion. It depended on where they had stood, whether they happened to be protected by some obstruction or had, indeed, been buried under a brick wall. It depended on their constitution and age as well as on various other circumstances which all made a difference to the way in which radiation sickness attacked them and to the length of time they survived.

One day a sister who had been lying beside Sister Mizoguchi died. Only a few days before she had said that she was all right. She had no evident injuries and no symptoms of the disease. But this very same sister – who had seemed so healthy, had nursed the injured, prayed to God in their last moments and buried them in the ground – was all of a sudden marked by dark-red congestive spots. The interior of her mouth began to bleed; suffering from nausea and bloody diarrhoea, she was sick again and again.

121

'Ah! It was the same with the dead Elizabeth!' she cried. She was struck with horror. Four or five days later she also died, just like those she had buried.

Many died. Those who lived buried the bodies and then, in a little while, the same symptoms in turn appeared in them. Therein lay the real and fearful terror wrought by the atomic bomb, and it continued for over forty days.

From Josei Girls' School to the top of Motohara, there was a path that led all the way uphill. While the sisters suffered and died in the air-raid shelter at the foot of the hill, the shadow of death ascended this path. The Maekawa family, the Matsuokas, and then the Yamaguchis, were attacked by radiation sickness from about 20 August. From then on, those people who lived lower down the hill began to be carried on the backs of others up the path to the hospital.

Even where two people had been in the same place when the A-bomb exploded, the same symptoms did not necessarily develop in each of them at the same time, or in the same way. It seemed that the younger members of each family had the least resistance to the disease and died the sooner. On the other hand, should they manage to get over the worst, the sooner they sometimes got better.

The day after one young girl died, her elder sister began to lose her hair. Crying over the younger sister, she said: 'I now have all the same symptoms as she had. I'll surely die.'

Her father, suffering from similar symptoms, looked down at his daughter sadly, already resigned to die – a sequence of despair that lasted forty days.

I named this widening advance of the disease the 'concentric circle of death'.

On 25 August, a hospital patient who had lived near the Yamaguchi house died. The very next day, another man who had lived in a house 100 metres further up the hill was on the brink of death. The circle of death, spreading out from the epicentre, ascended the hill towards our hospital.

Anxiously I watched my colleagues. Each day, towards the end of August, I gently tugged at the hair on the heads of the chief nurse, Miss Fukahori, and Miss Murai, as well as of those around me – to check their state of health. All of us were suffering from nausea to a greater or lesser degree; we felt dreadfully tired and had diarrhoea. But we kept this secret from each other. Brother Iwanaga, Mr Noguchi, Mr Shirahama, Mr Matsuda, Mr Ueki, Mr Kawano and I said nothing about our symptoms. But I took constant notice of the appearance of the hospital staff and made a point of pulling their hair to reassure myself they were all right. Meanwhile, death inexorably mounted the hill towards us.

Another member of Mr Yamaguchi's family died. He had lived in a house half-way between Josei Girls' School and the hospital. His home had been wrecked, but not entirely, since it was partly shielded from the blast by a shoulder of the hill. Mr Yamaguchi had been working in the Mitsubishi section of Nagasaki's shipyards, where the world's biggest battleship, the *Yamato*, had been built, when the atomic bomb exploded at 11.02. He hurried homewards, but his house was on the other side of the burning city. It took him all day to find his way around the fires, walking over the hills. When, at last, he reached his house he found all his family unharmed. He thanked God for this deliverance and set to work, clearing up the debris of his shattered home, out of which he erected a wooden hut, a temporary shelter of planks.

Within six days one of his family was attacked by radiation sickness and died a few days later. After 15 August, another member was attacked, and died before long. Great demands were made on Mr Yamaguchi, the strongest person in his family. He not only nursed these two who fell sick, but also, when they died, tried to give them a proper burial. He went to the cemetery to dig their graves; he sent for a priest. After the bodies were buried, he came home exhausted. Then a third member of the family caught the disease, sickened and soon died.

It seemed as if the makeshift hut in which the Yamaguchis lived was completely in the grip of death's evil hand. Within it, the surviving members of the family lay face to face with the hideous facts of atomic disease and approaching death. Now and then, when I could, I called upon the family, but stood there helpless, incapable even of sorrow, stunned by the indescribable scene of their anguish.

It seemed as if Mr Yamaguchi had abandoned all hope and

could feel no sorrow. A man will behave most strangely when he is full of grief and fear. He said: 'They are dying, one by one. We are all going to die. Who will send for the priest when I am dying? Who will dig my grave when I am gone?'

His house had been a large one, so several people evacuated from the town, more than ten in all, had been billeted on his family. He sat exhausted on the ground outside the hut. 'Doctor,' he told me, 'today I feel like digging my own grave and burying myself.'

I said: 'Well, death comes to all of us, and I expect I'll also be buried in mother earth before long.'

There was nothing else I could say.

In the end, after forty days, Mr Yamaguchi was left all alone, except for his old father. He had buried thirteen of his household with his own hands.

The gutted house of Mr Yamagami was situated about 200 metres above that of Mr Yamaguchi. Of Mr Yamagami's six children, the eldest boy had been killed in the ordnance factory where he worked as a volunteer. Another had been crushed when the house collapsed. His wife, when she saved the other four children, had been severely burnt. She was now in Urakami Hospital. Mr Yamagami himself was uninjured, and it seemed that his four surviving children had recovered from their injuries. But these charming youngsters, of primary and middle school age, were not destined to survive.

Growing children attending primary and middle school appeared to be most susceptible to radiation sickness. They were of an age when young people can easily be stricken by acute osteomyelitis which attacks the bone-marrow. They were also of an age to be vulnerable to the onslaught of radiation. Bone-marrow cells, which grow rapidly, divide just as rapidly, and there are many feeble cells among them. These can be destroyed by large doses of radioactivity. This form of the atomic disease manifested itself as medullary leukaemia.

Mr Yamagami's four children, having survived the A-bomb explosion, died one after the other. His eleven-year-old son died on 11 August; his twelve-year-old daughter on 16 August; and a month later, on 21 and 23 September, respectively, his two youngest daughters died.

Their mother's extensive burns had meanwhile suppurated.

Her fingers had been burnt to the bone as she frantically tore at the tiles of the wrecked and burning house to rescue her children. Towards the end of August she was smitten with tetanus. There was nothing we could do for her in the unhygienic conditions in which we lived and worked.

'Please try and save my wife, at least,' begged Mr Yamagami, again and again. But there were no antibiotics, nor any medicines that might have saved her. She also died. I felt utterly hopeless.

Thus, from the beginning to the middle of September, the shadow of death advanced up the hill towards the hospital like an incoming tide. We had no idea how far radioactivity had affected the body cells of the staff who were in the hospital when the bomb exploded and had remained there ever since. All of us suffered from diarrhoea and a discharge of blood from the gums, but we kept this to ourselves. Each of us thought: tomorrow it might be me.

In those days we knew nothing about 'fall-out'. But, of course, a large quantity of radioactive material must have been scattered on the ground and over broken buildings. There was more radioactivity near the epicentre than that caused by the gamma rays or neutron rays, which were radiated directly at the moment of nuclear fission.

The source of this radioactivity was the swarm of various corpuscular, metallic elements produced by nuclear fission. They were comparatively large in atomic weight, but minute in terms of size, and the time it took for them to fall to the ground varied considerably. Some fell on the ground like rain directly after the explosion; others drifted down like a mist. People thought this was some kind of poison gas. In fact, there was radioactive barium and strontium in those microscopic particles that floated down like snow and gathered in tiny radioactive heaps on the earth.

These were the 'fatal ashes' of the fall-out, those radioactive elements which, it was believed, would continue to radiate radioactivity for seventy-five years. We had no reason to begin with to be afraid of these fatal ashes; we were simply glad to have survived thus far. It was not until the concentric circle of death expanded, until our neighbours began to die of radiation sickness, that we became stricken with fear for the future. The staff, who had struggled for so long to look after those in their care, were now in turn seized, to lesser or greater degrees, by attacks of nausea, bloody diarrhoea and intolerable fatigue.

I myself felt far from well, especially after doing the rounds on foot of my patients all the way from Urakami Hospital to the lower part of Ueno town.

'I feel awful!' I said to Mr Noguchi.

On 25 August, the scorched leaves on the trees seemed abnormally green in the setting sun, and again against the clouds the following morning. To me it seemed an ominous sign; but no one remembers it now.

On the evening of 24 August, in Tokyo, General Tanaka, after drinking tea with his aide, went into his office in the next room, laid his ceremonial sword, his cap and gloves beside six carefully composed letters, already written and addressed, and sat in an armchair. A few minutes later he summoned his aide, and in his presence, shot himself.

On 25 August, the advance party of Americans who had planned to land in Japan on the 26th were prevented from leaving Okinawa by a typhoon. The flight of forty-five C47s was postponed for forty-eight hours. The planes took off with 147 men on board at 3 a.m. on Tuesday, 28 August, landing at sunrise on Atsugi airfield near Tokyo. Colonel Charlie Tench, one of MacArthur's staff in Manila, was the first American to step on Japanese soil. The occupation began.

Two days later, on 30 August 1945, a single plane, a C54 named Bataan, *landed on the airfield at 2.19 p.m. General Douglas MacArthur had come to take command of the conquered nation.*

5

On 28 August 1945, the Americans landed at Atsugi. I said: 'Japan has finally become one of the United States of America.'

My heart was filled with grief.

In our only newspaper appeared the picture of MacArthur, the Supreme Commander, standing on Atsugi airfield, striking a gallant pose. I read the paper squatting on some straw while cramming a ball of rice into my mouth. He stood fully six feet tall, with a clean-cut face and sunglasses, a corncob pipe in his mouth, wearing a simple military shirt and trousers of the same colour. He seemed to glory in his victory, as if this were the proudest moment of his life.

I looked at this picture of him and then looked around the yard. We were sunk in misery, yet the casual style of his shirt and trousers was more impressive than the photos of Japanese generals, who had always been prone to inspect their troops on horseback, covered in medals.

From this day on, a series of drastic changes would be made, steadily and surely altering the Japan we had known, destroying the old and creating what was new and hopefully good.

But at the beginning of September, when the American army were about to occupy Fukuoka and Nagasaki, wild rumours began to spread: 'I hear the cattle are all being killed and eaten by the American soldiers.'

'Let's kill all the cows and eat them ourselves!'

'Let's kill all the hens and finish them off!'

Rumours amplified in the telling. People who had been injured by the atomic bomb were easily frightened by the mere rustling of withered grasses, as if they were fugitive warriors. One rumour gave rise to another.

'Women and children had better flee for their lives.'

'The Americans will do what they like with the women and children.'

'Every woman should run away and hide!'

Such words spread like wildfire. Refugees began to flee from the city, heading for the hills.

'In two or three days the Americans will occupy Nagasaki – women and children should leave before they arrive.'

People living in Urakami fled towards Kawabira or Kobe; in their turn, those living there ran away to the deeper shelter of the mountains. For a few days there was total confusion. I wondered what they were trying to escape from when so much damage had already been done by the atomic bomb, when American troops and planes and tanks could easily pursue them into the very heart of the mountains.

I couldn't, however, help but feel uneasy when I saw women hastening past the hospital towards the hills, their belongings on their backs. In the hospital there were quite a few nurses, cooks and female patients.

I said to myself: Well, as for me, I don't care a bit what happens. But it might be safer for the women to get away.

One of the patients, Mr Aoki, said: 'American marines are crude and ruthless. We had better see that the women leave.'

I called the nurses and the cooks together and said: 'Tomorrow the Americans will arrive in Nagasaki. There's something I think you ought to do – I think you ought to leave. I couldn't endure it if anything terrible happened to you. You had better leave the hospital and seek shelter where you can.'

Some women from the neighbourhood had already fled. Now the in-patients and female staff began their own preparations to leave.

Miss Murai asked me, her eyes unblinking: 'What will you do now?'

I replied in a low voice: 'Me? I will stay here.'

'Then I'll stay here as well,' she said. 'I am a nurse.'

'You are a woman, and anyway, it's different with me. Go away.' I spoke to her bluntly. 'I'm a man, and what is more a doctor. Even the American marines won't harm those who've just died, or those who are about to die, or the doctor who tends them.'

The seriously ill tubercular patients and the sick and wounded looked up at me uneasily. The skin of some of those lying on the straw had turned black, some mulberry; others had pus all over their backs; one of the children was suffering from tetanus.

I said: 'Don't worry. I'm sure they won't hurt you. You've more than suffered as innocent servants of God.'

I tried to reassure them. I thought of protesting to the Americans when they arrived about the terrible suffering they had caused, accusing both them and their bomb of inflicting so much misery and pain, and telling them that they had to do something to save the lives of the survivors.

But, in the end, the nurses, cooks, theological students, in-patients and victims of the bomb, all decided not to run away and leave me alone in the hospital. They hadn't run away when the atomic bomb exploded, and even now, when the Americans were about to occupy Nagasaki, they chose to remain – not because they wanted to stay here with Brother Iwanaga and me, but because they trusted in the protection of the Virgin Mary and St Francis, who had long ago inspired the founding of both the mission school and the hospital.

The official ceremony of Japan's surrender took place on board the American battleship, Missouri, *on Sunday, 2 September – henceforth decreed by President Truman as VJ Day. The eleven-strong Japanese delegation, led by a Foreign Office minister, Mr Shigemitsu, and General Umezu, embarked on a dull and windy day from Yokohama at 7.30 a.m. and were taken on the destroyer,* Lansdowne, *out into Tokyo Bay, where the victorious American fleet was moored, dressed overall with flags. Escorted by three destroyers, which were laden with the world's press, service chiefs, statesmen and politicians of all the Allied Powers, the* Lansdowne *came alongside the* Missouri, *Admiral Halsey's flagship. The American flag flown by Commander Perry when he entered Tokyo Bay in 1853 had been brought from a naval museum and*

129

now hung from a bulkhead overlooking the scene. At 8.55, Mr Shigemitsu, short and bespectacled, in a top hat, high collar, tail-coat and dark striped trousers that concealed a wooden leg, hauled himself with the aid of a walking-stick on to the Missouri's *crowded deck. His delegation lined up facing a table – on which were the documents of surrender – and the massed representatives of the nations Japan had fought, and with some of whom she was still at war. The Americans were all dressed informally, in suntans and caps; no one wore a tie. At 9 a.m., General MacArthur, accompanied by Admirals Nimitz and Halsey, emerged and MacArthur read a prepared speech to the assembled and silent throng. It began: 'We are gathered here, representatives of the major warring powers, to conclude a solemn agreement whereby peace may be restored. The issues, involving divergent ideals and ideologies, have been determined on the battlefields of the world and hence are not for our discussion and our debate.' And it ended: 'It is my firm purpose, in the tradition of the countries I represent, to proceed in the discharge of my responsibilities with justice and tolerance, while taking all necessary dispositions to insure that the terms of the surrender are fully, promptly, and faithfully complied with.'*

Shigemitsu and Umezu signed where indicated. MacArthur used six pens to sign his name, pens that would be given to his family, friends, West Point and the National Archives. His signature was followed by those of the Allied representatives. Then MacArthur said: 'Let us pray that peace be now restored to the world and that God will preserve it always. These proceedings are closed.'

The sun came out as a flypast of B29s and many other American planes roared over Tokyo Bay.

The Allied Forces were most careful not to behave like victors when they occupied Japan. In particular, this was the case with the troops who first landed on the main island; they were especially considerate.

It was probably on 4 September that two foreign officers visited the burnt-out remains of our hospital.

I was in the basement when a nurse approached me and said: 'Some American officers want to see you, sir.'

'Well, I'm sure they're not going to kill me,' I said, and went out without any ceremony, dressed as usual in my dirty, dark-blue suit.

I came across the two officers, standing in a corner of the ruins. One was an American naval officer, more than six feet tall; he was a slender, handsome man, like a movie-star, with very bright eyes and a prominent nose. The other seemed to be Chinese. He may have been an NCO.

Taken by surprise at my sudden appearance, the second man put his hand on the pistol by his side, but, seeing me looking so shabby and no better than a beggar, he relaxed his hold on the pistol as if he saw he had nothing to fear from me.

The American was apparently a naval surgeon; he was very tall indeed: my face was just about on a level with the buckle of his belt. I had studied German at high school and university, but I had not studied enough English – I could read it well enough, but had difficulty understanding it when spoken, and couldn't speak it myself. The Chinese NCO appeared to understand some Japanese. He apparently found it difficult to believe that I was a doctor.

For a while the American walked around the ruined hospital, gazing with sympathy and concern at the survivors who lay here and there in the ruined wards. He seemed to be an eye specialist, for he began eventually to examine the patients' eyes with an ophthalmoscope, which could only be used by him putting his face close to that of a patient. Dropping on to his knees, he examined the eyes of those patients whose faces had been burnt and were badly inflamed and suppurating. In the case of those who were unable to sit up, he peered into their retinas, getting down on all fours to do so.

At first the wounded were uneasy about his intentions. But soon they began to relax, reassured by his kind but businesslike attitude. They thought that from now on they would receive some modern medical treatment, instead of the basic applications of zinc oxide oil, mercurochrome and Rivanol.

The Chinese NCO and I followed the American on his rounds. What he said was interpreted by the Chinese NCO, who used medical terms in English, not in German. Thus I was only able to guess at what was being said.

The American remarked: 'Most of them have had the optic

131

nerves of their retinas damaged by the A-bomb's flash, and their eyesight has been impaired. They may even lose it altogether.'

I shuddered, reminded of that brilliant white flash. Lose their eyesight? Surely he didn't mean that. Then I remembered observing a solar eclipse through a sooted piece of glass when I was a schoolboy. Children who used such a glass were safe enough, but those who observed the eclipse directly were warned that their optic nerves might be permanently damaged.

It was just as I had thought: the white flash had been as bright as that of the sun.

The American said: 'The cornea has been injured in many cases, causing a purulent corneal ulcer. It has been ruptured, and they may lose their sight because of this. The fact that they are lying in such insanitary conditions doesn't help. Why don't you send them to the first-aid station set up in the city centre?'

I roughly understood what he was saying, connecting his words to his gestures. But I wondered how far I could make him understand me. The interpreter couldn't interpret any Japanese medical terms.

I said: 'The survivors used to live in this neighbourhood; their houses were burnt down and members of their families killed or seriously injured. They aren't able to go down to the first-aid stations in the city. I was the chief doctor here. I was here when the atomic bomb exploded, but luckily wasn't hurt. However, the hospital, with all its equipment and supplies, was burnt down, as you can see. If you would be good enough to provide me with some adequate medicines, I should like to stay on here and continue with my treatment of these people.'

I repeated myself to this effect several times, for I was not sure how much he understood of what I was trying to say.

He said: 'Well, they have medical supplies in the first-aid station in the city centre – you should go there tomorrow and see what you can acquire.'

From the day the Americans came to Nagasaki, they brought in large quantities of medical equipment and opened a relief station in the ruins of Shinkozen Primary School. A medical relief hospital was also set up by the Medical Relief Headquarters of the Nagasaki City Medical Association. Most of the members of the Medical Relief Headquarters were doctors whose houses had also been burnt and whose families had been A-bombed.

Before this, at Yamazato Primary School, and then at Ibinokuchi, first-aid stations were also set up. But the one at Shinkozen Primary School was the first full-scale relief hospital. Plenty of new, highly efficacious drugs and medicines, such as penicillin, plasma and sulphur diazin were stored there by the Americans. They were so wonderful that the Japanese doctors, who had been left far behind during the Second World War by the medical advances made in America and Europe, coveted them greatly.

Urakami Hospital was about five kilometres from Shinkozen Relief Hospital. Although it wasn't far, it seemed to me and to the survivors of Motohara to be as much as a hundred kilometres away. Between, lay the area devastated by the A-bomb. Urakami Hospital was, in fact, about 1·6 kilometres north of the epicentre.

I was much impressed by the good-looking officer who had come on his own initiative to our hospital and inspected the eyes of the injured. He had made me aware of what was good in America. It now seemed absurd that we had been terrified of the marines and thought that women should flee from them.

The next day I set out for Shinkozen Relief Hospital in high spirits. I trudged along in my shabby dark-blue lounge suit, with a pair of worn-out shoes on my feet – I had managed to borrow them after my sandals fell apart.

Reaching the hospital at last, I found it to be piled with crates of penicillin, plasma and so on. They were in the custody of a pharmacist. Somewhat nervously I went up to him and said: 'Yesterday an American officer came to the Urakami Hospital and told me to come here to get some medical supplies. So here I am.'

The hospital official was not too keen on sparing me some of his medicines and put on a long face. 'Send your patients here,' he replied.

I had neither the inclination nor patience to describe the situation in my hospital and merely repeated my request. He seemed to accede to it. I looked enviously at the splendid new drugs of various kinds and the crates and the boxes with English writing on them. I coveted them, but in the end I just took what I was given: a small amount of sulphur – sulphaguanizine, useful for bowel diseases – and returned to Motohara, greatly depressed. All I could do was to go on feeding the patients unpolished rice and miso soup and urging them to take lots of salt.

After the American officer's visit, our wretched hospital, standing on the fringe of the devastated area, slipped from the minds of those who came to investigate the damage done by the atomic bomb. It went unprovided with the new drugs and the help that they could bring. Those who came to see what had become of Nagasaki after the A-bomb explosion stopped at Matsuyama town and Urakami, and never found out what was happening up on the hill of Motohara.

At the start of September, signs of the approach of autumn gradually began to appear. Goose-grass sprouted in the city, transformed into a wasteland since 9 August, and the flies were everywhere. It would soon be the 210th Day since the start of the Chinese new year, and the beginning of the typhoon season. That year was the Year of the Rooster.

We looked up at the sky and thought about the long, hot, painful summer, as if it had happened a long, long time ago.

On Sunday, 2 September, light rain began to fall.

'Oh, at last!' said Miss Murai. 'Here comes the rain – it's been so long.'

At first it was just the kind of rainfall that had, in the long spell of hot weather, been longed for by those who had suffered from the heat for over twenty days. But now it kept raining all day long, turning into a tropical downpour on the night of the 210th Day.

That night I listened to the heavy rain cascading down on the ruined hospital, on the scorched fields. Outside, in the utter darkness, the rain descended in torrents. The hospital staff gathered together in the store-house. Towards midnight, the rain came down harder and harder.

'What a terrible downpour!' I said. 'I'm very worried about the patients and the wounded lying in the ground-floor rooms.'

I went out into the pelting rain accompanied by the chief nurse and Miss Murai. The ruined walls of the hospital inside as well as out were streaked with the streaming rain. On the concrete levels of the wrecked wards on the ground floor, 110 A-bomb survivors lay attended by their families, while most of the hospital in-patients lay in the basement, wrapped in thin coverlets. The gutted roof had long since collapsed and the windows been blown out; but the floor-levels had stood firm, the second floor taking the place of a roof and protecting everyone from exposure to the rain. But the building had many windows, and the rain poured in from both sides and down the walls, and the injured gradually gathered in the middle of each ground-floor room in bunches of ten or fifteen, covering themselves with pieces of cloth, huddling together like small birds in a nest, folding their wings and sheltering from the storm. I never imagined a house without doors and windows could make me feel so sad.

'Doctor, what will become of us?' they cried. 'How heavy it is – we have hardly ever had such heavy rain. But still we're quite fortunate to be here, for we have, as it were, this double roof made up by the floors above us.'

This heavy rain lasted from 2 to 3 September and flooded the whole of Nagasaki. There wasn't a single house in Nagasaki city that was proof against the rain; for even the houses that had remained standing had lost their tiles and had their windows broken. The townspeople were thus visited by one misfortune on top of another. But the areas devastated by the atomic bomb suffered most from the rain. Dug-out shelters were washed away by water streaming down the hills; the planks and corrugated-iron roofing of lean-tos collapsed. Everything seemed to be under water. The scanty clothes, the furnishings, the bits and pieces that people had salvaged, were all saturated by the rain. The damage to possessions didn't bother me so much as the fact that the sick and injured were also being soaked to the skin. Twenty days before some of them had been badly burnt; others had suffered severe injuries. Since then they had struggled on, despite their wounds and sickness, in the midst of total destruction, and after much difficulty had managed to build some makeshift shelters in dugouts or under overhanging banks. But now all were washed away by the rain and the people were drenched to the skin. Hadn't they suffered enough? Not content with the destruction brought by the atomic bomb, was heaven going to torment them further with water? It was a new kind of hell on earth – torture by fire was being followed by water-torture. I looked up at the sky and shouted: 'Don't punish them this way – it's too much! Haven't you done enough?'

On the afternoon of 3 September the downpour lessened. And then it stopped.

The 4 September turned out to be a fine, cool, autumn day. The temperature had dropped. In the early autumn sunlight I went out to see those of my patients who dwelt in the neighbourhood. Wet mats that were rotting away had been slung over broken walls to dry. In the sunshine, the survivors of the atomic bomb were laying out their clothes, their bedding, the boards and bits of furniture that now formed their houses; they even stood in the sunshine to dry themselves. In spite of the misery caused by fire and water, humanity clung tenaciously to life.

The rainfall during those two days was of a heaviness we had rarely experienced in Nagasaki. The Meteorological Observatory recorded more than 300 millimetres of rain.

After the rain, Urakami Hospital was in a very bad way. On the second floor, which served us as a roof, great pools of rain water had formed themselves into a lake. This water gradually soaked through the concrete and down on to the floor below. Soon pools of water spread on the first floor and began leaking through to the ground-floor level.

Although the weather was now fine out of doors, the leakage of water continued from the second floor down to the ground. Water dripped endlessly on to the survivors, and the ravaged and burnt-out hospital wards, along with the injured they contained, became wet and damp. Although the sun shone outside, inside the hospital it seemed to keep on raining.

The sound of water dripping in the wards went on for days after those two days of heavy rain. In the darkness of the ruined hospital I would listen to the sound in deep sadness.

'Something's happened!' I said to Miss Murai. 'I feel there's a change in the air – I'm sure of it.'

Going out on my rounds after the heavy rain, I looked at the earth beneath my feet and at the surrounding hills and took a deep breath. Somehow I felt refreshed, and it was not only because of the fine weather of early autumn – there was something else. The sick feeling in my stomach had begun to disappear. I thought: The world has changed.

I had no machines or equipment to measure the change; no

one had any geiger-counters. But, since 9 August, having walked every day on the scorched earth and shattered tiles, I now felt convinced there was something different about the ground as well as in the air.

'That's it!' I said to myself. The poison has been washed away!

The people were thinking ill of merciless heaven as they dried out their few possessions. But the heavy rain had, in fact, proved to be nothing less than a merciful act of providence. In the area destroyed by the A-bomb no creatures had been destined to live for seventy-five years. But the rain now proved to be the vital element that brought everything back to life. The torrential rain that had flooded the city had washed the deadly radioactive ashes into the ground or out to sea.

At the end of August, when the people were utterly confused and greatly disheartened by the news of the end of the war and the occupation of Japan by the Americans, the council of the faculty of medicine in Kyushu University had been undecided about whether or not to send an investigatory commission to A-bombed Nagasaki.

Some said: 'I don't think the time is right to send anyone there. First of all, we should re-establish order in our university.'

Professor Sawada said: 'On the contrary, Hiroshima and Nagasaki were devastated by atomic bombs; Kumamoto has also been extensively damaged. Our university hasn't been touched. It is the responsibility and duty of every doctor to do what he can to heal the sick and wounded in these cities.'

It was several days before the council accepted Professor Sawada's recommendations. He had also thought that Japan, by gathering scientific data concerning the A-bomb disasters, might indict America before the world for its barbarity while the Americans were boasting how civilized they were, how just and how free.

The commission, consisting of pathologists, physicians, forensic experts, zoologists and nuclear physicists, the élite of each department, duly arrived and began their investigations on 8 or 9 September. They discovered Nagasaki to be in a far greater state of misery than they had imagined.

The deputy mayor of Nagasaki asked them to establish as soon as possible whether human beings would be able to survive in future in the area devastated by the atomic bomb. The people had heard that no one would be able to live in Nagasaki for seventy-five years, and their worst fears were confirmed when members of families died one after the other of radiation sickness. Wild rumours spread through the ruins, as fearful as the stench that issued from the wreckage, where everything that had not been burnt to cinders continued to decompose and decay.

The commission from Kyushu University encountered many difficulties. They had never had to deal with such quantities of radioactivity and radiation sickness. An unknown world confronted both the doctors and the investigators. They had no idea where to begin or exactly what to do. They were short of young doctors and were very short of supplies. They made medical examinations of the bomb victims as well as of those who had come to their rescue, such as relatives and medical teams. But they had only one microscope.

At first, in 25 per cent of those examined, the leucocyte counts (counts of white blood cells) per cubic millimetre of blood were startlingly low, the count for a normal person's blood being between 5,000 and 10,000. But they discovered that a month after the A-bomb explosion, the percentage of people whose leucocyte counts was under 1,000 greatly decreased to 3 per cent. In addition, in none of the rescuers was any leucopenia, as the condition of white blood-cell deficiency is called, to be detected.

Only 200 or 300 people were examined, but the commission soon reached a number of bold conclusions which the heavy rain of September helped to ratify. For if there had been no rain, then the dramatic fall in the number of leucopenia sufferers, in my opinion, would not have taken place.

On 10 September, the commission tentatively published the results of their investigations, reached without much sleep or rest. Showing the detailed scientific data obtained, they stated that the radioactivity produced by the atomic bomb was not strong enough to prevent people from living in the city, thus scotching the rumour that no one would be able to live there for the next seventy-five years.

The report on Hiroshima, published at about the same time by Professor Sagane, a nuclear physicist at Tokyo University,

138

said much the same. He stated that there was little long-term danger to life since the radioactivity had sunk deep into the earth and would only be gradually released.

Mr Naruse, the deputy mayor of Nagasaki, was greatly relieved at these conclusions. He stated that the commission's report would be one of the motivating forces in the reconstruction of Nagasaki. In fact, this report was, from a scientific point of view, rather a rough-and-ready piece of work, but in such a state of emergency it was necessary for a decisive conclusion to be reached quickly. However, its accuracy was in part reinforced by the providential rain that fell in the first few days of September and by the Makurazaki typhoon.

General MacArthur entered Tokyo on Saturday, 8 September. He had stayed until then in Yokohama. A mighty parade of American forces and armour moved through the ravaged city, ultimately all but encircling the Imperial Palace. MacArthur drove to the American Embassy, where another ceremony was enacted. A band played 'The Star-spangled Banner', and then he said: 'Let our country's flag be unfurled, and in Tokyo's sun let it wave in its full glory as a symbol of hope for the oppressed and as a harbinger of victory for the right.'

The Stars and Stripes rose over the capital city of the Land of the Rising Sun.

Each day the sun shone and the sky was bright and clear. Day by day the goose-grass became thicker; cicadas and crickets could be heard again. It was cool in the morning and at night, but I could still hardly bear the heat of the day. There were swarms of flies.

The concentric circle of death had widened as far as a point about 100 or 200 metres away from the hospital.

I was told: 'The commission from Kyushu University are working at full stretch.' And the idea flashed across my mind that I could go and work with them, calculating leucocyte counts. However, the men and women who were my responsibility continued to fall sick and to die one after the other. Those who were seriously injured were not willing to go and see the doctors

139

from Kyushu University. They preferred to remain in the care of Catholic priests, from whom they could receive holy communion and be given their last rites before they died.

On the afternoon of Sunday, 16 September, the weather suddenly changed. It soon became overcast and grey rain-clouds swept in from the east. In the evening there was a storm. Although it was past the 220th day, when storms were believed to occur, it was still the season for them. No weather forecast had, however, prepared us for what was to follow.

After dark it began to rain in earnest. Unexpectedly, a cold autumn wind arose and swept through the city.

Mr Noguchi asked me: 'Do you think the in-patients and the injured should be left where they are?'

'Well, they may get wet,' I said, 'but this building has solid concrete floors and ceilings, and they'll be better off here than anywhere else. We're all tired – let's have a good rest.'

I repeated these words to the brothers and the nurses and to the sick and injured who lay in the store-house and in the ground-floor rooms.

'Doctor, it's raining and blowing very hard!' said the patients in some anxiety.

I cheered them along, saying: 'Well, seeing how the hospital wasn't destroyed even by an atomic bomb, I'm sure it will be proof against the heaviest storm.'

Then I lay down to sleep in the basement bathroom.

Before long the rain began to descend in cataracts. The east wind grew to a gale, howling and raging about the hospital in the dark. The noise of the storm increased and the rain splashed down like a waterfall. I wondered if this could be the onset of a typhoon.

'Doctor, please could you come to the wards on the ground and first floors,' said a nurse, standing in the doorway, dripping wet.

'What's the matter?'

'All we can hear is the patients crying in the dark.'

I went outside. It was blowing much harder than ever. I couldn't keep myself upright – the rain and the wind beat me sideways.

Two of the brothers and I swiftly inspected the ground and first floors, on which the injured had been redistributed since the recent heavy rain. The great three-storeyed concrete building, now a mere skeleton, seemed to be shrieking in the blasting wind and rain. I heard the cries of the injured coming from the darkness: 'Doctor! Help! Do something to help us!' Their voices were drowned by the roar of the storm.

The building, being without window panes or frames, was equally as vulnerable to the driving rain as one without a roof, for it had many large windows. The wind had shifted and rain was now being dashed into the rooms through the windows on the northern side. Already the first floor was almost flooded.

The injured had been accommodated in half-burnt iron beds since the previous heavy rain. These now stood in pools of water that were straying all over the floor. The rain poured through the windows in torrents, hurled by the wind. I felt as if I were on the bridge of some storm-tossed ship and was being drenched by wind-driven waves.

'Doctor, help me!' pleaded a patient.

'All right, I'll take you down to the basement,' I shouted.

'I can't possibly move,' said the injured man.

He was reluctant to move because the burns on his body hurt him. The wind and the rain became more and more violent, streaming through the windows on the north side of each room. The patients couldn't stay where they were, but where could I take them? Their bodies were burnt and ulcerated – they suffered much pain. I was totally at a loss. There was the kitchen, but it had also been swamped and was piled with food supplies. Besides, it would be impossible to carry all the injured on stretchers as far as the kitchen.

The hospital had been built as a sanatorium for consumptives. In earlier days we had made a mortuary in the basement, where memorial services were also held. It had remained undamaged when the hospital caught fire because the ceiling and walls were made of concrete. But it was littered with wooden panelling, screens and plaster, torn down by the pressure-blast of the A-bomb – there wasn't even an empty space in which one could stand. Besides, it was hardly a happy place for me or the nurses, because when a patient died his body would be laid there for the night. But the room did face south and was in the basement; it was not directly exposed to the wind and rain of the typhoon raging out of the north-east, and so far no water had leaked into it. In other words, there was nowhere in which the patients might shelter from the violence of the storm, except for the mortuary itself.

'Let's carry them to that room!' I exclaimed.

'That room? What do you mean?'

Mr Noguchi and Miss Murai stared at me in puzzlement.

'*That* room,' I repeated. How could I say – 'the mortuary'?

The brothers and nurses brought stretchers. We began to carry the sick and injured down to the mortuary, stumbling in the dark, lashed by wind and rain whose ferocity was ever increasing. The windowless, roofless hospital was no less exposed than the bridge of a ship battered by the raging waves of a storm at sea.

'Doctor, help me!'

'Doctor!'

The injured cried out in the dark.

'We're going to move you down to the basement!' I shouted.

Miss Murai began lifting a wounded man on to a stretcher. He cried out. Having been burnt on his back, his arms and thighs, the slightest touch caused him pain. One of the theological students tried to move another man, but he also cried: 'Awh! Ah – no!' It was impossible to move him. He gave a cry of pain and said: 'I don't want to move. I'll stay here.'

'You *can't* stay here! We must take you down to the basement.'

I shouted at them in the midst of the howling wind and rain. The sick and injured wailed and cried. It seemed as if we would never even get them on to the stretchers. The storm screamed about us. There was no time left. I was, as it were, the captain of a sinking ship.

'Stand up! On your feet! Get on the stretcher by yourself!'

The patient stared at me astonished.

'Stand up! On your feet!'

He stood up, in spite of himself.

'Now, move yourself on to the stretcher!'

He began to move, fearfully. Though a touch on his arms or his legs caused him pain, he got up and moved on to the stretcher by himself.

The brothers, the nurses, the students and I, wet to the skin, persuaded and moved each patient on to stretchers, then carried them down to the mortuary.

'Doctor, is this to be our new sickroom?'

They saw it had been a mortuary. They felt like crying all the more.

'There isn't anywhere else we can put you!' I said, as if I were angry, and ordered them to be laid on the floor of the mortuary. How could we be so unkind?

But we kept on transferring the patients, one at a time, in the wind and rain. Everyone was wet through. My loud voice and the patients' cries were overwhelmed by the noise of the storm and rain. A terrible necessity had overcome the limits of the spiritual endurance of the nurses, students and brothers. We desperately moved the wounded, sipping the rain that ran down our faces. We moved about thirty patients.

We were past blaming the storm, the atomic bomb or the Americans who had dropped it on people who were men and women like themselves. This did not mean that I, for one, accepted the fact of surrender. I was only afraid that any desire for retaliation would cause further grief and pain. I was afraid, above all, that my mind could become unbalanced by endless resentments against others. That night we passed the limits of endurance, with the rain pelting down and streaming mercilessly into our mouths.

During the night the storm veered and grew even more violent, raving above us, but at last it passed over. No warning of its approach was issued at any time by the Meteorological Observatory or the radio.

For the third time the people of Nagasaki suffered. The makeshift huts which they had managed to rebuild were again blown down and torn apart. Roof-tiles and sheets of corrugated iron were whirled away by the wind. Cooking-pots left in front of hovels were nowhere to be found next day. People cursed their cruel lot and reproached the merciless heavens.

This typhoon was one of the worst Japan had experienced for many years. It traversed Kyushu from south to north, striking first at Makurazaki, then at Shimabara and Nagasaki, before speeding between the prefectures of Yamaguchi and Hiroshima to the Sea of Japan.

I was told later that the typhoon tore through Hiroshima causing even more damage than it did in Nagasaki. In Hiroshima a study group sent by the faculty of medical science at Kyoto University had been investigating the damage caused by the

143

atomic bomb; Professor Mashita headed the group. Since there were no lodging houses, they had put up some tents at the epicentre and were using them as laboratories in which to conduct blood tests and various clinical examinations. The typhoon swept through Hiroshima before dawn on 17 September. The study group's tents were blown down; Professor Mashita was killed. Life seemed to be worth nothing more than a leaf or a straw at the mercy of the wind. Now we had surely suffered enough. 'No more!' I cried.

In the morning after the typhoon abated I felt somewhat refreshed, relishing the cool, invigorating breeze that blew after its passing. Along with the others in the hospital, I dried my clothes in the sun. I felt the same as I had after the heavy rain on 2–3 September – no, I felt even better.

The flies had disappeared; the hot weather had gone. Nearly all the remnants of that fatal radioactive fall-out had now been washed away or carried deep into the earth. I had no means of measuring radioactivity, since I had no geiger-counter; accordingly, I was unable to compare the counts before and after the typhoon. Later, however, various study groups who visited Nagasaki reported that a little radioactivity remained for a while at Nishiyama. But they confirmed that it *was* possible for those of us who had survived the bomb to go on living in the city. None the less, if Japan had known as little rain as the deserts of Nevada or Arizona, what would have become of us? We owed our deliverance to a typhoon, to the heavy rain that comes with the changing seasons to Japan.

People often say in Japan: 'Kamikaze, the divine wind, will blow.'

Kamikaze was the historic typhoon which, when the Mongols invaded our islands, blew and destroyed the enemy. During the Second World War our military leaders had told us: 'The divine wind will blow very soon and save Japan from this wretched state of war.' But during the war, the divine wind, Kamikaze, never blew. The typhoon after the atomic bomb attacks was our Kamikaze, which saved the people from secondary effects of radioactive fall-out.

After the typhoon, the death toll suddenly decreased near the

144

hospital; the advancing tide of death retreated and sank like water into the ground. The staff and I recovered from our feelings of nausea, from the symptoms of radiation sickness.

From that day on, the apparent inevitability of death was transformed into a reassertion of life. We did not know why this should be so, but the daily fear that we would all soon die, gradually diminished as, day by day, autumn turned into winter and the year came to an end.

The dead were dead; but those who survived could start to live once more.

That September, three men returned to Nagasaki and walked through the city over which they had flown on the morning of 9 August 1945. Chuck Sweeney, Don Albury and Kermit Beahan had come to see what 'Fat Man' had done. The city was still a place of horror – of desolation and devastation, of bodies, bones and blackened and shattered buildings and homes; the city stank. They walked through the wreckage, where survivors lived in improvised shelters, unimaginably maimed in body and mind, still scratching around for family remains in the ruins while dying themselves. They looked away as the conquering airmen passed, and perhaps, as the three Americans looked about, their eyes rested for a moment on the distant ruined hospital on the hill of Motohara.

Postscript

Gordon Honeycombe

Thirty-five years after the A-bomb exploded above Nagasaki I visited the city, in June 1980, to find out more about Dr Akizuki, the city and the bomb.

Before the war, the city was generally known in Europe and America for one thing; it was the home of Madame Butterfly. A statue of her stands in the lush gardens of a westernized bungalow that once belonged to Thomas Glover, an English industrialist who introduced weapons and warships to Japan in the 1860s. He grew rich and married a Japanese girl, Tsurujo, which means 'Crane'. Not as pretty a name in western ears as Cho-Cho, 'Butterfly'. But the fact in Nagasaki as elsewhere is not always as pretty as the fiction. Mr Glover's charming residence, identified now with Butterfly's house, was built on the weapons of war. But it was here, you are invited to imagine, that Butterfly, on the veranda overlooking the harbour, sang that passionately lovely lament. 'One fine day,' she sang, 'we'll see a thread of smoke arising . . .'

Anyone looking north from Mr Glover's garden at 11.02 a.m. on 9 August 1945 would have been smitten by a scorching light, a sound of thunder and a hot blast, and two miles away would have seen a fireball, like a small sun, flowering above the Urakami valley before dissolving into the mushroom cloud of the brave new nuclear age. On that day some 30,000 people died, most within minutes of the flash, crushed by collapsed buildings or burnt to death. The facts are these: unprotected skin was singed up to 4 kilometres away from the epicentre; timbers and textiles were scorched as far away as 3·5 kilometres; people up to 1·2 kilometres away and out of doors received fatal burns, which caused 25 per cent of all deaths; a third of the city, 6·7 square kilometres, was reduced to ash and ruin; 50 per cent of the energy released by the plutonium bomb's explosion produced a colossal wind-blast, while 35 per cent resulted in a flash of heat and 15 per cent in radioactive rays. Within months, the number of deaths more than doubled, people dying of burns, injuries and radiation sickness. In the thirty-six years since then, the death toll has risen to nearly 100,000, and people are still dying from the merciless unseen after-effects of the bomb.

The plutonium bomb dropped on Nagasaki, equivalent to 22 kilotons of TNT, was potentially much more destructive than the 13-kiloton TNT equivalent of the uranium bomb detonated over Hiroshima. The resulting death toll there, also about 100,000, is, as in Nagasaki, higher than the present official figure of around 78,000, and much higher than earlier American and UN estimates. There are still no accurate and up-to-date figures of A-bomb casualties. But more than 96,000 names, of those who died because of the bomb, have so far been recorded in the Hiroshima Memorial. The Nagasaki figure is slightly less (although the plutonium bomb was more deadly) because it exploded in the geographical confines of northern Nagasaki, not over the harbour area. If it had done so, the destruction and death toll would probably have been much greater, as the fireball's heat and blast would have spread over and up Naga-saki's two main valleys, not just the one, and the houses on the hill where Thomas Glover's home still stands would have been cast down and set ablaze – not the homes like Mr Yamagami's on Motohara hill.

The terrible chances of that day are legion, centred on the fatal significance of the actions and whereabouts of every person in the Urakami valley during the forty seconds that the A-bomb fell from the sky. The ironies are as grim: the bomb was dropped in the wrong place at the wrong time, for it would never have been released over Nagasaki if the target at Kokura had been visible – and it was almost never dropped on Nagasaki because of the weather. But Kokura lived and Nagasaki died. Since then, ironically, Kokura has been wiped off the map – not by a cataclysm, but by urban development. No large-scale map shows Kokura now: it has been swallowed up by the metropolitan sprawl of Kitakyushu. Now Kokura has gone – Nagasaki yet lives.

So does Mitsubishi, a multi-national, multi-million-pound business empire, whose presence in Nagasaki in 1945 (shipyards, steel works, ordnance factory and so on) made it a suitable target for an atomic bomb. Mitsubishi thrives and prospers; the company logo, three red propellers, shines in the night sky over the city, and is seen all over Japan and around the world. Nagasaki's most famous, most successful child is now Mitsubishi, not Madame Butterfly.

I asked a town hall official what was directly beneath the bomb when it exploded. I discovered it was a tennis court, set in a broad garden surrounded by trees: 171 Matsuyama town – the bungalow, or second house, of a wealthy industrialist, Mr Takami. He was connected it seems with the Mitsubishi Company, and some weeks before the bomb exploded had sold or loaned the property to Mitsubishi for use as a hostel for girl students working for the company. On 9 August, the house had not as yet been occupied – it was empty. How ironic, I thought, that the bomb's erroneous eventual target should have been the least important but latest acquisition of the Mitsubishi Company – Mr Takami's tennis court.

Nagasaki now is not much to look at, pleasant and lively though it is. Little that was old survived the war and the bomb, and what has been rebuilt because of the bomb or city planners, is undistinguished and functional, much of it obscured by the gaudy advertisements, banners and signs that obliterate buildings in every Japanese centre of commerce, while the streets, rattling with single-decker tram-cars, are webbed with power cables and wires. But everything is clean and cared for; the people are epitomes of industry, courtesy and good cheer; and the service, as elsewhere in Japan, must be the best in the world. Yet the standard of living is low, and most things are expensive, even local produce. What appealed to me was the absence of tipping even in the air-conditioned taxis, all tips being added to the fare or bill. What also appealed was that the Japanese drove on the left, as in Britain, and although I was a foreigner and very tall, they never stared. Neither they nor I seemed alien. There was something about their good-mannered reserve that was endearingly old-fashioned and almost British.

Perhaps island peoples, like the Japanese and British, being industrialized though rural, great travellers though insular, have something in common. Their humour seemed British, as well as their middle-class aspirations and deceptions, their facial diversity, their fondness for flowers and gardens, for children, for sport, for clubs and societies, for holidays abroad, for keeping up with the Japanese Joneses and keeping oneself to oneself. Their TV programmes were as well made and as varied as those in Britain, although a higher percentage were educational and baseball dominated sport. Yet there were moments of unease. On TV one night I chanced to see a sickening sequence of clips from American horror films, including the climax of *The Texas Chain-saw Massacre*, which were being shown to a studio audience composed entirely of teenage girls. Then I read in an English-language Japanese paper about the unveiling in a Tokyo public park of a memorial honouring seven Japanese leaders who had been executed after the war by the Allies as war criminals. In connection with this, I noted a remark made by a high-school teacher about the mooted American bequest to the Japanese army (euphemistically called the Self-Defence Force) of nuclear weapons. 'They must not be given these,' said the teacher. 'Otherwise they will *use* them.'

There were other disturbing moments: when the sirens that had once warned of air-raids wailed in the city, announcing the start and end of the working day – when hotel musak tinkled out tunes like 'Oh What a Beautiful Morning', 'Feelings', 'On a Clear Day', 'The Last Waltz'; when two giggling schoolgirls asked me to pose with them for a photograph on the balcony of the A-bomb Museum.

I had been self-consciously gazing at huge photos of the actual A-bomb explosion and 'Fat Man', a model of which is now on display in New Mexico; *Bock's Car*, the B29 that dropped the bomb, is on show at an airbase in Ohio, with a boastful mushroom cloud now painted beside the winged boxcar on its fuselage. Seeing such photos among the many grisly relics of the museum made one feel ashamed of being a westerner.

I felt abashed, however, for the Japanese, when I saw the giant bronze Peace Statue in the Peace Park, now gone pale green – a seated, grossly muscular westernized man with eyes shut, supposedly a buddha – pointing with his right hand to heaven and stretching the left out over the earth, thus indicating, I was told, whence came the bomb and whence and where God's peace is spread. The statue's incredible hulk appeared to me to be like the grotesque fantasy of some mad American general, its posture and distorted proportions signifying nothing but the triumph of the bomb.

The apparent insensitivity of the Japanese struck me more than once – as much as their evident sensitivity about social values. I was saying good-bye to the headmaster of a high school. School was over for the day. The smartly uniformed pupils were now earnestly engaged in all sorts of sporting and musical activities. Suddenly the opening phrase of 'The Star-spangled Banner' rang out mockingly on a distant trumpet. It was repeated several times. I was told there was no American camp next door – some pupil was practising on his trumpet. But why the American national anthem? Because, I was told, the sequence of notes made an excellent trumpet exercise. Very practical. But I winced, hearing that conquering phrase repeated in Nagasaki.

It seemed to me that the Japanese had learned to love their conqueror – that having been vanquished for the first time ever, and so completely, they had abandoned the precepts that led to their defeat and adopted those of the victor, believing them now to be best. Certainly over the last thirty-five years they had most diligently studied American methods and the workings of democracy, and had learned very fast and well. They have also done quite well out of the twenty-year occupation by the Americans of Japan (130,000 servicemen are still stationed there), and out of two American punitive wars, those in Korea and Vietnam. Unfortunately, their national identity has been diluted and pervaded by their contact with and desire to emulate the American way of life, to the extent that hamburgers, chips, rock music, baseball, records and gangster movies seem to be the main preoccupations of the young. Moreover, the Japanese desire not to offend has become a vice vis-à-vis the Americans, to the extent that the Japanese play down the casualties caused by the atomic bombs and by other bombing and overplay the culpability of their own leaders in prolonging the war. The

150

Japanese would even seem to be embarrassed about having been atom-bombed.

In Nagasaki they obscure the fact with an improbable Peace Statue, by calling the A-bomb Museum an International Cultural Hall and disguising it as a five-storey block of council flats, by camouflaging the dark-green pillar that marks the explosion's epicentre against a background of dark-green trees, and by hiding the few surviving mementoes of A-bombed wreckage among the bushes and trees of a shabby, unweeded garden, as it was when I was there.

However, apart from optimistically selling cigarettes with brand names like 'Peace', 'Hope', and 'Partner' – and they seem to be as favoured as American brands – the Japanese desire for peace seems to be real enough. A recent poll in the United States and Japan asked the inhabitants, 'What would you do if your country were invaded by a foreign power?' In America, 72·8 per cent said they would fight. It was 20·6 per cent in Japan. There is also a vigorous Peace Movement in Nagasaki, led by the Mayor, and a late but growing concern for the welfare of the *hibakusha* (A-bomb survivors) whose suffering is unprecedented in world history. For a generation they have suffered and still they suffer from the delayed physical and social effects of the bomb – from skin growths, cataracts, leukaemia, cancer, malignant tumours, microcephaly of foetuses, general debility, premature ageing, as well as from discrimination, poverty and the disintegration of family life. A total of 390,000 people in Japan are accredited *hibakusha*, and the financial aid given to them annually now amounts to more than 8,400 million yen. It is still not enough, and the Peace Movement would like the Japanese government to pass a new law that fully compensates all *hibakusha*. The movement, opposing any nuclear developments in Japan, also campaigns for world peace and nuclear disarmament, and does what it can to promote peace education in every school, despite much official opposition. Their idea is that if this becomes a basic principle in education, if pupils understand the inhumanity and cruelty of war, recognize the causative forces at work and think positively about the achievement and maintenance of peace, then the chances of a nuclear holocaust must decline.

This idea is good and practical. But there is more that might be done. The Mitsubishi Corporation could assume some responsibility for the welfare of the *hibakusha* in their former company town – and the United States for all the rest. The Japanese government could and should publish an up-to-date, definitive account of all the facts and figures concerning the A-bomb explosions and exert themselves as the peace-makers of the world. And Nagasaki city might honour more fully those who died through the atomic bomb by establishing nobler and more exalting memorials than those that now exist.

In the meantime, at 11.02 a.m. on 9 August every year, the sirens wail again in Nagasaki and people stand still, remembering that day the bomb exploded a generation ago. Pupils at many schools in Nagasaki, but not all, are recalled from holiday and reminded about what happened in their city long before they were born. Ceremonies of remembrance and services are held in churches and hospitals as well as in schools. The one in the Peace Park is attended by many survivors, including one or two ex-prisoners of war, who stand among their former enemies, all *hibakusha*, observing a minute's silence. Not as many will be there this year, but probably more than next. For the younger generation are largely indifferent to the lessons of the past and some people do not care to remember. The survivors diminish, winnowed by age, by the long-term effects of the bomb. Before long, people will say: 'Why bother?'

I go to see Dr Akizuki.

On the way from my hotel to Motohara, the air-conditioned taxi passes on my left the vanished POW camp, new Mitsubishi factories, the railway line, and on my right the tree-hidden epicentre – the Peace Park laid out on the site of the once annihilated prison – and the still uncompleted concrete towers of Urakami Church. The taxi climbs through narrow streets, past post-war buildings crammed together, giving no hint of their tormented foundations, and suddenly it turns right on the hill of Motohara into a forecourt green with ornamental palms and bushes and centred on a larger than life-size white statue of St Francis. And I find it impossible to believe that here, where a large and spacious white modern hospital building now stands, St Francis Hospital, caring for 200 patients of all kinds, there once were the burnt-out tragic wards of Urakami Hospital, destroyed by an atomic bomb that exploded on a level with the hill less than a mile away.

Dr Akizuki is the principal, now as then.

After exchanging my shoes for a pair of slippers, as is usual in some institutions as well as in Japanese homes, I am greeted by two sisters of the Order of St Francis, for the hospital is now supervised by nuns. They are garbed in white; they take me into an ante-room furnished with wide mock-leather settees confronting each other across a long wooden table. The high window is hung with floral net curtains, and a flower arrangement on a stand decorates a corner. Sister Marysia is tall and American, wears glasses, is earnest and lady-like, not unlike Lady Churchill; she speaks Japanese. Sister Veronica is Japanese, small, bespectacled, oval-faced and ever ready to smile; she speaks very good English. Between them they will act as interpreters, as Dr Akizuki's English is not too good, helping each other, translating my questions and his replies. Outside, it begins to rain.

Before long Dr Akizuki appears, wearing the short white coat of a doctor. It is something of a shock to see him, now aged sixty-four, alive and apparently so well, having read his story half a world away and several worlds removed from his experiences. He can hardly be more than 5 feet 1 inch and is startlingly slight: he must weigh 9 stone or less. He wears glasses, and looks like a sprightly, grey-haired, aged boy. He grasps my hand warmly in both of his and says: 'Welcome to Japan. I am happy to see you. You are *very* tall!' He grins, much amused. Looking down at him from my 6 feet 4 inches, I wonder if he recalls that very tall American officer, the naval eye-specialist, the first American he saw after the war ended. He sits down on the low settee opposite me, and the sisters range themselves beside him. I gather his health is poor: his chest is weak; he has to rest in the afternoon. But he is still busy in the hospital, and his emphatic replies and gestures belie his frailty. He sits relaxedly at the settee's end by the window, leaning on an arm, contemplating me through his glasses. Now and then he beams, and I find myself looking at his glasses, not at his eyes, as if they might transmit what they have seen.

Conversation is slow, as questions and replies are translated into English. Sister Marysia, when she speaks, has a habit of prefacing her words with a soft-spoken, 'See . . . Now see.' I have time for thought, time to be smitten by the strangeness of the situation. The rain pours down. Green tea is brought and sits in little cups on the table between us. I am given an ice-cold Coke.

No, says Sister Veronica when she understands my question – no nightmares. Dr Akizuki doesn't have nightmares now. But after the war they were made afraid by thunder, by sirens; their hearts stopped, remembering that day. Dr Akizuki adds something in Japanese, gesturing widely, his voice full of force. Sister Marysia translates. When he sees movies or TV, she says, when he sees people escaping, running away, that reminds him of the bomb, very badly; this he cannot stand. 'No watch,' says Dr Akizuki, 'I go.' He nods and smiles. He understands some English but is reluctant, like most Japanese, to seem ignorant or foolish in using it wrongly himself.

I learn to my surprise that Sister Veronica was also in Urakami Hospital when the bomb exploded. She was then Miss Kataoka, aged sixteen, a trainee nurse. Now she is a Sister of St Francis and the hospital's administrator. Dr Akizuki attributes their survival to the drastic diet he forced on everyone in the hospital – salt with everything, and no sugar, nothing sweet. He speaks further; Sister Veronica translates: 'He say he believe we have a mission, to tell what happen here . . . That is why he feel God give him life, to live until now.' He is active in the Peace Movement, and revered, as I found, for what he did and still does. He is the director of the Nagasaki Association for Research into Hibakushas' Problems.

He feels no bitterness against the Americans. He would rather blame the Japanese government for prolonging the war. He says they *knew* Japan must lose the war, but they did not bring it to an end. If they had capitulated earlier, the atomic bombs would never have been used. The people, he says, felt the war should stop; there was no hope of winning. Yet even after Hiroshima, the government still would not surrender, claiming that Japan would win in the end – and if not, then all would die.

Recalling that the Christian community in Nagasaki, mainly Catholic, was a large one, then and now, I ask him whether the deaths of those who were killed by the bomb might be regarded as a sacrifice: they died that others might live. He says he doesn't

154

think like that, although some do and did. He is now a Catholic himself, like his wife, having been converted a few years after his marriage. I inquire after Mrs Akizuki: where does she live, and what does she do? I am told that she will be here in a moment, and it transpires that she was also in the hospital on the day of the bomb, one of the nurses. She was working with the doctor when . . . 'Miss Murai!' I exclaim, amazed and delighted. I remember that scene of the interrupted pneumo-thorax operation in the consulting room . . . 'Miss Murai.' No – I am corrected – Mrs Akizuki.

Now I want to know what happened to the other survivors. They tell me. Dr Yoshioka, whose face was badly cut, still lives near the hospital and is now in her seventies; Miss Fukahori, the chief nurse, died ten years ago; Father Ishikawa returned to Korea, became a bishop and died there recently; Brother Joseph Iwanaga still teaches in the rebuilt theological college; Mr Noguchi is now a Franciscan priest and the bishop of Utsonomiya Church, sixty miles north of Tokyo. Miss Murata, the injured kitchen-helper, married and left Nagasaki. Mr Matsuda, one of the seminarians, died in 1946. Mr Kawano, who escaped from the burning medical college, is a brain surgeon and the head of a municipal hospital in Kitakyushu. Of those friends and neighbours who were injured, Mr Yamano, whose leg was injured by a falling tree, is now over eighty and confined to bed with a blood complaint; Yokichi Tsujimoto rebuilt the family home, remarried, became a baker and a city councillor, concerning himself with social welfare, and died of cancer when he was seventy-two. Mr Yamada, one of the two carpenters badly injured when the air-raid shelter they were constructing collapsed, lived on until 1970, building many houses; Mr Yamaguchi remarried and is now a butcher; Mr Yamagami, whose wife and six children died, lives alone in his reconstructed house across the road from the hospital.

Mrs Akizuki comes into the ante-room, a charming, slim, ascetic-looking woman in grey, with glasses, her still-dark hair tied in a bun at the back of her head. She smiles a lot and, producing a camera, begins taking snaps of her husband and me. I learn that they were married in 1949. Dr Akizuki is not too sure of the exact date; Sister Veronica giggles. He became a Catholic a few years later. The Akizukis have two daughters, both at university; they are fit and well, but sometimes their father is afraid of what might happen. After the war, all he thought about was the present: it was all that was important. Life was difficult then, he says, and he was very tired and sickly. Miss Murai was the one person he thought he needed, and after they were married she wanted children. They only lived for the day.

It has stopped raining. Dr Akizuki leaves the room to exchange his white coat for a jacket. I ask his wife whether their shared experiences after the A-bomb brought them together. She is abashed – she doesn't know – she thinks not. Then Sister Veronica translates a considered reply. Maybe the bomb did.

Dr Akizuki returns in his dark-blue business-suit, carrying an umbrella half his height. We go for a walk, crossing the road outside the hospital. On the damp, heavily built-up hill he points out where the Tsujimotos used to live, where Mr Yamagami still lives, in an old-style Japanese house with blue tiles. 'Yamagami!' shouts Dr Akizuki from the path above, but there is no response. A cemetery lies further up the path, a cemetery distinguished by its tall dark memorials and decorative trees, silhouetted against the grey sky. Here the ashes of Mr Yamagami's wife and six children are preserved, their deaths commemorated in red and gold on a dark pillar topped with a cross. Further on is the war memorial to the nuns of the Convent of the Holy Cross. Here also is a small plaque commemorating the death of Dr Akizuki's sister. He looks very tired and solemn; his frailty shows.

I ask him if he has any message for the West. He says: 'The progress of human knowledge, science and morality, created the atomic bomb – we must not forget this fact.' 'But,' I ask, 'is progress good or bad?' He replies: 'That is the question.'

As I leave, he smiles reassuringly, clasping my hand with both of his. 'Peace,' he murmurs. 'Peace.'

Extract from the Farewell Address
to the Nation made by President Carter
on 14 January 1981

It has now been 35 years since the first atomic bomb fell on Hiroshima. The great majority of the world's people cannot remember a time when the nuclear shadow did not hang over the earth. Our minds have adjusted to it, as after a time our eyes adjust to the dark.

Yet the risk of a nuclear conflagration has not lessened. It has not happened yet, but that can give us little comfort – for it only has to happen once.

The danger is becoming greater. As the arsenals of the superpowers grow in size and sophistication and as other governments acquire these weapons, it may be only a matter of time before madness, desperation, greed, or miscalculation lets loose this terrible force.

In an all-out nuclear war, more destructive power than in all of World War Two would be unleashed every second for the long afternoon it would take for all the missiles and bombs to fall. A world war every second – more people killed in the first few hours than all the wars of history put together. The survivors, if any, would live in despair amid the poisoned ruins of a civilization that had committed suicide . . .

Nuclear weapons are an expression of one side of our human character. But there is another side. The same rocket technology that delivers nuclear warheads has also taken us peacefully into space. From that perspective, we see our earth as it really is – a small and fragile and beautiful blue globe, the only home we have. We see no barriers of race or religion, or country. We see the essential unity of our species and our planet; and with faith and common sense, that bright vision will ultimately prevail.

Recommended Reading

The Records of the Atomic Bombing in Nagasaki, published by the city of Nagasaki, 1975.

Report from Nagasaki, edited and published by the Nagasaki association for research and dissemination of *hibakushas'* problems, 1980.

The Fall of Japan by William Craig, published by Weidenfeld and Nicolson, 1968 and Pan Books, 1970.

The War Against Japan (Official History of the Second World War) by Major General S. Woodburn Kirby, published by H.M.S.O., 1957.

History of the Second World War by B. H. Liddell Hart, published by Cassell, 1970 and Pan Books, 1973.

The Second World War (illustrated) by A. J. P. Taylor, published by Hamish Hamilton, 1975.

The Second World War (6 vols) by Winston S. Churchill, published by Cassell, 1948–54.